De tous biens plaine

Recent Researches in Music

A-R Editions publishes seven series of critical editions, spanning the history of Western music, American music, and oral traditions.

Recent Researches in the Music of the Middle Ages and Early Renaissance
Charles M. Atkinson, general editor

Recent Researches in the Music of the Renaissance
James Haar, general editor

Recent Researches in the Music of the Baroque Era
Christoph Wolff, general editor

Recent Researches in the Music of the Classical Era
Eugene K. Wolf, general editor

Recent Researches in the Music of the Nineteenth and Early Twentieth Centuries
Rufus Hallmark, general editor

Recent Researches in American Music
John M. Graziano, general editor

Recent Researches in the Oral Traditions of Music
Philip V. Bohlman, general editor

Each edition in *Recent Researches* is devoted to works by a single composer or to a single genre. The content is chosen for its high quality and historical importance, and each edition includes a substantial introduction and critical report. The music is engraved according to the highest standards of production using the proprietary software MusE owned by MusicNotes, Inc.

For information on establishing a standing order to any of our series, or for editorial guidelines on submitting proposals, please contact:

A-R Editions, Inc.
Madison, Wisconsin

800 736-0070 (U.S. book orders)
608 836-9000 (phone)
608 831-8200 (fax)
http://www.areditions.com

RECENT RESEARCHES IN THE MUSIC OF THE MIDDLE AGES AND EARLY RENAISSANCE, 36

De tous biens plaine

Twenty-Eight Settings of Hayne van Ghizeghem's Chanson

Edited by Cynthia J. Cyrus

A-R Editions, Inc.
Madison

A-R Editions, Inc., Madison, Wisconsin
© 2000 by A-R Editions, Inc.

All rights reserved. No part of this book may be reproduced or transmitted in any form by any electronic or mechanical means (including photocopying, recording, or information storage and retrieval) without permission in writing from the publisher.

The purchase of this edition does not convey the right to perform it in public, nor to make a recording of it for any purpose. Such permission must be obtained in advance from the publisher.

A-R Editions is pleased to support scholars and performers in their use of *Recent Researches* material for study or performance. Subscribers to any of the *Recent Researches* series, as well as patrons of subscribing institutions, are invited to apply for information about our "Copyright Sharing Policy."

Printed in the United States of America

ISBN 0-89579-475-6
ISSN 0362-3572

∞ The paper used in this publication meets the minimum requirements of the American National Standard for Information Sciences—Permanence of Paper for Printed Library Materials, ANSI Z39.48-1984.

Contents

Acknowledgments vii

Introduction ix

   The Origins of the Repertory ix
   The Music x
   Performance Considerations xiii
   Notes xiii

Text and Translation xvii

Plate xviii

Twenty-Eight Settings of *De tous biens plaine*

The Original Version 3

   1. De tous biens plaine *(a 3)*, *[Hayne van Ghizeghem]* 3

Si Placet Settings 6

   2. De tous biens playne *(a 4)*, *Anonymous* 6
   3. [De tous biens plaine] *(a 4)*, *Anonymous* 10

Substitute Contratenor Settings 14

   4. De tous biens playne *(a 3)*, *Anonymous* 14
   5. De tous biens plaine *(a 3)*, *Anonymous* 17
   6. De tous biens *(a 3)*, *Anonymous* 20
   7. De tous bien *(a 4)*, *de Planquard* 23
   8. [De tous biens plaine] *(a 4)*, *[Josquin des Prez]* 27

Settings Based on the Superius 31

   9. De tobiens plena *(a 3)*, *Anonymous* 31
   10. De tous biens *(a 3)*, *Josquin [des Prez]* 34
   11. De tous biens *(a 3)*, *[Johannes] Ghiselin* [dit *Verbonnet*] 37
   12. De tous biens playne *(a 4)*, *Anonymous* 40
   13. [De tous biens plaine] *(a 3)*, *Anonymous* 44
   14. De tous biens *(a 4)*, *Anonymous* 47

Settings Based on the Tenor 51

   15. [De tous biens plaine] *(a 3)*, *Anonymous* 51
   16. De tobiens plaine e ma maetressa *(a 3)*, *Anonymous* 54
   17a. De tous biens *(a 4)*, *[Alexander] Agricola* 57
   17b. [De tous biens plaine] *(a 3)*, *[Alexander Agricola?]* 61

18. De tous biens *(a 3), Anonymous*   64
19. De tous biens *(a 3), Bourdon/[Alexander Agricola]*   67
20. De tous biens playne *(a 3), Alexander Agricola*   70
21. De tous biens playne *(a 3), Alexander Agricola*   74
22. De tous biens playne *(a 3), Allexander [Agricola]*   77
23. De tous biens playne *(a 3), Allexander [Agricola]*   80
24. De tous biens *(a 3), Bactio [Bartolomeo degli Organi]*   84
25. De to biens playne *(a 3), Anonymous*   88
26. De tous bien plen *(a 4), Anonymous*   94
27. De tous biens *(a 4), Jo[hannes] Japart*   99
28. De tous biens plaine *(a 4), D'Oude Schuere*   103

Critical Report   107

List of Sources   107
List of Works Cited   109
Editorial Methods   110
Critical Commentary   111
Notes   120

Acknowledgments

I owe an intellectual debt to Howard Mayer Brown, whose listing of chanson settings of various sorts in his *Music in the French Secular Theater* first sparked my interest in this project, and to Honey Meconi whose ongoing conversations about the process of reworking material have helped to shape my own thoughts on the place of the fifteenth- and early-sixteenth-century "arrangement." I am also grateful to Alice Clark, Laurel Zeiss, and Elizabeth Randall Upton, who have served as sounding boards at various stages of this project. The Music Division of the Library of Congress provided the plate from the Laborde Chansonnier under complicated circumstances; thanks to Jon Newsom and especially to Margaret Kieckhefer and Bill Parsons for facilitating the reproduction. Thanks go to the many libraries that supplied microfilms for this study; they are listed among the sources for the settings in this edition. I would also like to thank the Musicological Archives for Renaissance Manuscript Studies of the University of Illinois at Urbana-Champaign, the University of Chicago, and the Newberry Library for allowing access to their microfilm collections. Special thanks go to various librarians who were generous with time, advice, and interlibrary loan requests: Ida Reed of the University of North Carolina at Chapel Hill, and Shirley Watts and Cheryl McClure of Vanderbilt University. This research was supported by a Vanderbilt University Research Council Grant and by a Newberry Library Consortium Fund Award.

Introduction

The Origins of the Repertory

The family of musical settings based on Hayne van Ghizeghem's *De tous biens plaine* ranks among the largest groups of related compositions stemming from the fifteenth and sixteenth centuries. Although not as prestigious as the more famous complex of *L'homme armé* masses, nor perhaps as long-lived as the settings based upon Johannes Ockeghem's *Fors seulement*,[1] the *De tous biens plaine* family is notable for the range and breadth of its chanson-to-chanson transformations, a repertory identified here as "chanson settings."[2] These settings explore a variety of approaches to the model, but traditionally excerpt a single voice, either superius or tenor, and interweave newly created polyphony around the borrowed line. Although one might consider such settings derivative, they were evidently prized in their own day, for they abound in the chansonniers from the late fifteenth and early sixteenth centuries, where they exist side by side with the other varieties of chanson types that flourished at the turn of the century. In fact, chanson settings comprise approximately one-fifth of the surviving secular repertory from the last decade of the fifteenth century, and they remained popular until the development of the Parisian chanson in the 1520s. A complete inventory of this repertory has not been attempted, but in her study of the twelve largest families of related settings, Honey Meconi has identified nearly 150 individual chanson settings, many of which exist in multiple copies.[3] Thus, if the number of models and arrangements in notated sources is any indication, *De tous biens plaine*, along with other families of related settings such as *Fortuna desperata*, *Fors seulement*, *J'ay pris amours*, and *D'ung aultre amer*, must have been among the most recognizable musical materials in the courtly repertory.[4]

The model for the *De tous biens plaine* settings, itself one of the most widely circulated chansons of the entire fifteenth century, remains one of the best-known works of its day. At least twenty-six copies bear witness to its immense popularity, and it also inspired a half-dozen intabulations as well as allusions in plays and poems.[5] The earliest exemplars of Hayne's rondeau quatrain fall in the 1460s and 1470s and belong to the so-called Franco-Burgundian manuscripts, while other copies from the same decades stem from Savoy and Naples. Since the earliest copy of *De tous biens plaine* is found in Wolfenbüttel,[6] a source copied in the first half of the 1460s, the chanson must have been one of Hayne's earliest works. His career, lamentably hard to trace, began a mere decade before with his training as a young boy in 1452 at the expense of Charles, Count of Charolais (who became Duke Charles the Bold of Burgundy in 1467). Hayne is documented at a Burgundian court banquet held in 1462 at which he played *bas instrumens* and sang with Robert Morton, and again as a singer and chamber valet at the Burgundian court in 1467. While he drops from the documentary record after the siege of Nancy in December 1476, the date of his death is unknown, and some scholars believe that he was still active as late as the early 1490s.[7]

That the circulation of *De tous biens plaine*, Hayne's "greatest hit," started with Burgundian associations, then, is unsurprising, but the explosion of copies in the 1480s and 1490s is perhaps more remarkable: by 1500, there were at least eighteen copies of Hayne's original song in circulation, including Florentine and northern Italian copies.[8] The arrival of Hayne's *De tous biens plaine* in Italy is matched by the appearance of seven chanson settings in Florentine sources from the 1490s, works which rank among the earliest of the chanson-to-chanson transformations in this family.[9] During the remainder of the song's career, Hayne's original setting continued to vie with its musical progeny in the chanson sources. The 1500s witnessed its expansion to four voices—in Petrucci's *Odhecaton* (setting 2) and in Bologna Q18 (setting 3), for example—and the publication of various arrangements, including ten additional settings published by Petrucci in the first four years of the century.[10] The sixteenth century also saw the arrival of both model and settings in more remote regions, including England and especially

Germany, where model and settings were copied as late as the 1530s.[11]

The composers who chose to rework Hayne's original setting extended into the so-called Josquin generation of composers, flourishing in the decades which frame the turn of the sixteenth century. Given their distribution in the sources, most of the anonymous settings also date from before or around the turn of the century.[12] The principal composers of settings were themselves well traveled: Franco-Flemish composers Johannes Japart and Johannes Ghiselin, dit Verbonnet, both worked at the court of Ferrara, Japart under Ercole d'Este in 1477–81 and Ghiselin in 1491 and 1503.[13] Similarly, the most notable composers to address Hayne's model, Alexander Agricola and Josquin des Prez, both had strong reputations in Italy as well as France, and the surviving renditions of their works are distributed across the two areas.[14] Lesser-known figures such as de Planquard and Bactio (Bartolomeo degli Organi) from Florence and D'Oude Schuere from the Low Countries were likely associated with the region where their unica settings survive.[15] Given the geographic distribution both of composers and of manuscripts and prints, it is probably best to consider the popularity of *De tous biens plaine* as a pan-European phenomenon, rather than as an expression of Franco-Burgundian hegemony.

Significantly, the array of surviving settings of *De tous biens plaine* suggests a less self-consciously competitive approach to the model than is seen with other families of settings. Nearly half of the settings survive anonymously. Moreover, unlike the triumphant mass cycles of the *L'homme armé* tradition or the competitive one-upsmanship[16] suggested by the clusters of *Fors seulement* and *J'ay pris amours* settings in some manuscripts, the *De tous biens plaine* reworkings tend to exist as single settings. Multiple arrangements only appear in Petrucci's collections, where the readings are widely scattered, separated by folio after folio of unrelated material, and in a cluster in Segovia. In short, this family does not seem to provoke the intense compositional competitiveness of *Fors seulement* or *L'homme armé*, for the compilers of these many manuscripts and prints were often content to include one or two versions as representatives of this particular song tradition. In this way, *De tous biens plaine* proves to be more stylistically representative of the chanson setting in general, for like many of the smaller families of reworkings, it lacks the obscure technical manipulations drawn forth by competition.[17] A few settings invert or transpose the borrowed voice, but most are content to include it without change, focusing their stylistic innovations on the added voices. Thus, the family of *De tous biens plaine* settings partakes in a conservative compositional practice in which the composer amplifies upon the model by weaving "new lines over, under and around [the] given cantus firmus" in a technique that Howard Mayer Brown compares to the "scholastic glossing on authority," a technique firmly grounded in the medieval polyphonic tradition.[18]

The Music

Hayne's rondeau (setting 1) displays the sinuous and long-breathed melodic lines typical of his generation; the first phrase, for instance, is fifteen measures long. The superius and tenor form the traditional discant-tenor framework, harmonically self-sufficient without the contratenor. Each of the major cadences which mark the ends of lines of text (mm. 15, 28, 41, and 60) and all of the subsidiary cadential gestures that occur midphrase (mm. 5, 22, 34, and 47) fall between the superius and tenor; together they form the necessary harmonies of major sixth to octave or minor third to unison, and one or the other voice establishes the pre-cadential suspension. There is no contrapuntal imitation in the Hayne setting, but the final phrase does involve motivic repetition: the rising figure in the superius of measures 42–43 is briefly repeated at the start of the next clause, measures 48–49. The tenor momentarily supports this repetition with its rhythmic delay in both spots, but Hayne's contratenor treats the two phrases quite differently. It helps to establish a clear-cut start to the final phrase by coordinating with the superius in measure 42, but it links together the two clauses at measure 48. In all three parts, most of the melodic motion is by step, with occasional leaps of a third or fourth. Similarly, the breve, semibreve, and minim (transcribed here as whole note, half note, and quarter note) account for most of the rhythmic motion, although the chanson's most familiar motive, the signature descending tetrachord with the rhythm of dotted semibreve-semiminim-semiminim-semibreve/breve which forms part of the superius's incipit, occurs several times and in all three voices (in the superius at mm. 2, 20, 30, 34, and 39; in the tenor at m. 22; and in the contratenor at m. 32).

Seven settings retain the discant-tenor framework of Hayne's version, two of which are si placet versions that merely add a newly composed altus to the three original voices.[19] The altus of setting 2 is actually labeled "si placet" in its sole surviving source, Petrucci's *Odhecaton*.[20] Setting 2 is probably older than the other si placet version, setting 3, for the altus of setting 2 moves at roughly the same speed as the other voices, occasionally providing rhythmic animation at cadences. The unlabeled altus of setting 3, on the other hand, proceeds much more vigorously, moving in minims and semiminims for most of the setting. There are a few uncomfortable moments in setting 3, notably the conflicts between superius and altus at the end of the piece. The unresolved major seventh in measure 51 might be explained away, since the superius has an appoggiatura and the altus fits the implied harmony. The passage in measures 57–58, however, is irredeemably awkward and has been emended in the transcription. The source has the altus arriving on the pitch A at the start of measure 57 and sustaining it for a measure and a half (with a breve and semibreve) before moving to G on beat three of measure 58. This harmony at the start of measure 57 proves unworkable, for the traditional superius has a B♭–C–B♭ pattern at this point, and the editor has adjusted the altus reading to minimize the dissonance. The thinly disguised parallel octaves (A to G) in the following measure have, however, been left intact. It is possible that setting 3 had a newly composed superius as well as altus, for the facing page is missing from the source, but this scenario is unlikely, for no other known setting in any family preserves the tenor and contratenor without also using the superius. Most likely, then, the superius of setting 3 was slightly varied, or the surviving altus is corrupt in spots.

The three settings that provide a substitute contratenor to the original version adopt remarkably different strategies. Setting 4 offers an old-fashioned, slow-moving contratenor with archaic octave-leap cadences; it also exhibits an unusual harmonic emphasis on C in the first phrase. Setting 5 uses a more typical mixture of rhythmic animation and motivic play (e.g., mm. 18–21), but it also adds an extended passage in triplets in the second half of the piece. Setting 6 expands on those features: it exploits a variety of semiminim motives and incorporates a condensed triplet passage to form a lively and wide-ranging rendition of the song.

The final pair of discant-tenor settings are the canonic settings by de Planquard (7) and Josquin (8). Each adopts a canon at the minim in the lower register, in place of the original contratenor. To accommodate the relatively rapid harmonic rhythm, the canonic voices move fairly systematically in semiminims, although longer values occasionally appear. The difference in tessitura between the two versions makes Josquin's the more approachable of the two settings for modern ears: the Josquin canon works mostly in the octave below middle C, while the de Planquard setting repeatedly returns to gamma ut, the low G, giving it a grumbly sound. Nevertheless, the de Planquard version, with its jouncy rhythms and its disjunct but melodically-sensible contour for the lower voices, has an appealing rough-and-tumble quality that is captured especially well on viols.

The remainder of the settings borrow a single voice from the model; settings 9–14 use Hayne's superius, while 15–28 employ Hayne's tenor. Most of the settings incorporate the borrowed voice without change, but in a few instances (settings 14 and 25–28) the borrowed voice is modified. Setting 14 adds occasional ornaments to the cantus prius factus in the superius, perhaps reflecting improvisatory practice. It also distracts attention from the superius by incorporating frequent voice crossings with the newly composed contratenor. Textural play, particularly imitation, between the upper two voices establishes the piece as a progressive setting. In comparison to the relatively minor changes made to the borrowed superius line, the modified tenor settings transform their cantus prius factus more extensively. Setting 25 employs cantus firmus technique, using a verbal canon to slow the tenor's motion relative to the already rapid outer voices. The outer voices of setting 25 are notable both for their extensive use of parallel motion and for the introduction of triplets (mm. 40–42). Setting 26 transposes the tenor melody up a fifth and places it in the superius, casting it above three brisk lower voices whose scalar figures at times overwhelm the cantus prius factus. Japart's approach to setting 27 follows his habit of manipulating borrowed materials, for he inverts the tenor and places it in the contratenor voice.[21] The final setting in this collection is the most unusual, for D'Oude Schuere transposes the cantus firmus up a whole step to A. The resulting modal shift creates a very different harmonic environment for the melody. Moreover, D'Oude Schuere adds ornamentation to the borrowed melody. These transformations of the original material, although typical in some other families of chanson reworkings, are unusual in the collection of *De tous biens plaine* settings.

The central portion of the *De tous biens plaine* repertory are the many settings drawing directly on either superius or tenor. The superius-based settings tend towards contrapuntal complexity. Setting 9 uses a process of motivic repetition in the newly composed tenor which Allan Atlas, following Tinctoris, dubbed *redictae*.[22] Each tenor motive is copied once and a bar line signals its repetition. These motives range in length from a single minim to three and one-half breves, with most motives hovering around a breve or two. Josquin contributes another canonic rendition in setting 10, this time forming a canon at the fifth. (This canon is not as tumultuous as that of setting 8.) Ghiselin's contribution, setting 11, although not canonic, does rely heavily on imitation in the lower voices. The anonymous setting 12 creates freer lower voices, but its contratenor is motivically obsessed, creating a series of ostinato-like figures. Of the traditional superius settings, then, only setting 13 lacks a contrapuntal motivation; it is a pleasant, uncomplicated work in which the new tenor proceeds a bit faster than the outer voices.

Two significant groups of tenor-based settings survive. The first is comprised of three related settings, one of which exists in two versions and all of which are distributed in Italian sources. Settings 15, 16, 17a, and 17b share not only Hayne's tenor but also an independent bassus motto that appears in the first two and one-half measures. Although it is not clear which version came first, the bassus of setting 15 has a sensible continuation which repeats the motive a fifth higher before moving on to new material. Setting 16 also incorporates motivic repetition at the fifth, but does so by placing the motto in the superius. The exchange of voices and the frequency of reduced texture in setting 16 make it a less likely candidate for a subsidiary model. The most widely circulated of the three related settings is the one by Agricola; setting 17a is a four-voice version found in *Canti C* with attribution, while 17b is a three-voice version of the same arrangement. The extensive passages of reduced texture in 17b suggest that the four-voice version was created first and the contratenor later stripped away. Note that Agricola's setting, like setting 16, makes use of the imitative placement of the motto.

A second group of tenor-based settings are also by Agricola, the only composer to contribute more than two settings of *De tous biens plaine*. Settings 19–23 display Agricola's fertile imagination. The first setting (19) actually has a conflicting attribution to Bourdon which is found only in the index to *Odhecaton* (and, curiously, not on the music itself). It is in some ways unlike the other Agricola settings, for the voices move in approximately equal rhythmic values at the beginning of the setting, although the new voices speed up in internal phrases and provide a slightly more rhythmically animated version than the model. The next pair of settings both employ scalar semiminim runs, but setting 20 also includes triplets (mm. 41–46), while setting 21 includes a significant and characteristic melodic sequence with a strong rhythmic profile (mm. 50–53). Setting 22 employs continuous minim motion in the outer voices; although they are not canonic, they exhibit the same spirit as the canonic settings by Josquin (settings 8 and 10) and de Planquard (setting 9), perhaps because the voices of Agricola's setting, like those of his contrapuntal colleagues, make use of disjunct motion in order to fit the harmonic scheme. The final Agricola setting (23) is the only surviving setting of *De tous biens plaine* to employ triple meter in the newly composed voices. Like its fellow compositions, however, it too demonstrates Agricola's emphasis on memorable rhythmic gestures, including syncopation, and on interesting textures, for it incorporates brief passages of imitation between the outer voices which help to unify the setting motivically.

The Agricola settings are preceded by another, more problematic, setting employing roughly uniform rhythms among the three voice parts, that of the suppressed version of *De tous biens plaine* from Bologna Q16 (setting 18). This setting, edited here for the first time, was apparently copied into the manuscript and then immediately suppressed by the expedient solution of gluing the pages together. This elimination of a unique setting occurred before the scribe numbered the pieces with roman numerals, for it bears no numbering of its own. The motivation for the piece's eradication may well have been the rhythmic errors in the superius part, for the work is virtually unperformable. No corrections are visible, suggesting that as the scribe read back over his work, he realized that editing the superius would be tantamount to recomposition in spots and so elected to eliminate the piece from the source. The modern-day editor is faced with a further challenge, for the glue has welded the pages together permanently.[23] This editor adopted the strategy of backlighting in order to transcribe the work, but notes that the reading of this piece is less certain than that of any other setting.

The Bactio setting (24), which follows the Agricola settings in this edition, retains and perhaps exaggerates the busy texture typical of an Agricola setting, for the new voices move fairly consistently in semiminims. The Bactio setting also incorporates triplet figuration not once but twice (mm. 8–14 and 41–46). Richard Wexler, who determined that Bactio was Florentine composer Bartolomeo degli Organi, suggested that this work might have stemmed from a sort of student apprenticeship with Agricola, for the features of Bactio's settings parallel those of Agricola's quite closely.[24] This accords with Brown's observations about the pedagogical function of modeling procedures. A novice composer could take the broad outlines of the compositional plan—features such as cadential goals, textural contrasts, or phrase length (as Bactio has done here)—and construct a new polyphonic complex incorporating those features.[25]

Two of the three incomplete settings which have been omitted from this edition share many of the characteristics of the settings edited here. The setting found on the first surviving page of Verona 757 (Meconi 6k) is presumably a three-voice, tenor-based reworking. Only half of the tenor and a newly composed bassus survive. The bassus proceeds at the slightly faster pace characteristic of the turn-of-the-century settings (e.g., 18 and 19). The missing superius might be a close variant of the original melody, for there are only a handful of spots where the original superius and new bassus clash, but they are distinctive enough to prohibit a "substitute contratenor" relationship. Likewise, the previously unidentified superius-based setting in Linz[26] now lacks a bassus, but a few stems along the bottom edge of the page attest to the presence of a third voice in the source. The surviving tenor employs a mixture of minims and semiminims and has a memorable profile. Both incomplete cantus firmus settings are aesthetically promising but unperformable in their current mutilated condition. The third fragmentary setting, on the other hand, appears to be far different in compositional plan than the other settings of this edition. The setting on folio 1r of Augsburg now contains a complete tenor and contratenor which are otherwise unknown.[27] The source was mutilated, probably for use as binding fragments, however, and only the lower remnants of the superius's first line of music remain. The surviving superius melody begins with the anacrusis to measure 27. Although the fragmentary superius clearly has the verbal incipit "Detous" and the piece follows the rough outlines of the harmonic plan of Hayne's setting, there is no clear-cut cantus prius factus. The superius seems to be a very loose and highly ornamented paraphrase of the original superius melody. The cadential gestures are reproduced in the new voice, but at times only the barest hint of the original melodic profile remains. Curiously, the melodic incipits in the tenor and contratenor voices resemble those of setting 13, and the fragmentary setting also shares with setting 13 the somewhat unusual arrival on a substitute B♭ harmony (B♭ + b♭ + d') at the medial cadence, but the two settings are otherwise unrelated.

Performance Considerations

Texting is perhaps the most vexatious issue for the performance of this repertory. Only six of the twenty-six copies of Hayne's original supply full text to the superius, yet the piece was probably originally intended for vocal or vocal-instrumental performance. Even in sources that provide the full text of the rondeau, only the refrain is underlaid; as is typical for the fifteenth-century rondeau, the remainder (*residuum*) appears in blank space elsewhere on the page. (See plate 1, where the *residuum* is written on the empty staves of fol. 62v.) The picture is further skewed towards untexted transmission for the reworkings; of the remaining settings, only one, setting 4, provides any text for the superius beyond the incipit, and it gives only the refrain text. Curiously, none of the surviving readings of model or chanson settings supplies any text beyond a simple incipit to the tenor part. Ultimately, however, this sparse use of texting in the sources may reflect a form of scribal abbreviation, for the text itself was well known and could presumably have been supplied by the singer. Thus, a texted performance of either superius or tenor is possible wherever a full performance of the rondeau is feasible, and in those instances the editor has supplied text in italics to facilitate vocal performance.

A variety of performance media would be appropriate for the performance of *De tous biens plaine* and its many progeny. An entirely vocal performance (with the contratenor and perhaps the tenor vocalizing on a neutral syllable) would be suitable for settings that retain the medial cadence, although a combination of voice and instruments or an entirely instrumental performance is equally viable for these settings.[28] Those settings that lack a clear-cut medial cadence or have a harmony which would not lead smoothly to the return of the A section are more likely to have been intended for instruments alone.[29] Period-appropriate performance would likely be restricted to one performer on a part, although instrumental doubling of a cantus firmus line in a setting is often a pragmatic compromise.

The tempo of the settings should be moderately fast. Although a "resting heartbeat" was considered standard, a slightly faster pace of 70–80 beats per minute, applied at the level of the semibreve (half note), is appropriate for nearly all of the settings.

Notes

1. The *Fors seulement* settings are available in *Fors seulement: Thirty Compositions for Three and Five Voices or Instruments from the Fifteenth and Sixteenth Centuries,* ed. Martin Picker, Recent Researches in the Music of the Middle Ages and Early Renaissance, vol. 14 (Madison: A-R Editions, 1981).

2. I am using the term "chanson setting" as a relatively broad category to cover a variety of three- and four-voice transformations of a polyphonic model that remain roughly the same length as the original. The term "setting" for such repertory has become standard; both Martin Picker in *Fors seulement: Thirty Compositions* and Honey Meconi in *Fortuna*

desperata: Thirty-Six Settings of an Italian Song, Recent Researches in the Music of the Middle Ages and Early Renaissance, vol. 37 (Madison: A-R Editions, forthcoming) rely on the term. The category excludes bicinia and combinative chansons. It also stands in opposition to the three- and four-part popular arrangements based on monophonic melodies. The latter repertory was first isolated by Howard Mayer Brown and further characterized by Lawrence Bernstein. See Brown, "The *Chanson Rustique*: Popular Elements in the Fifteenth- and Sixteenth-Century Chanson," *Journal of the American Musicological Society* 12 (1959): 16–26; idem, "The Genesis of a Style: The Parisian Chanson, 1500–1530," in *Chanson and Madrigal 1480–1530: Studies in Comparison and Contrast: A Conference at Isham Memorial Library, September 13–14, 1961*, ed. James Haar (Cambridge, MA: Harvard University Press, 1964), 1–50; idem, "The Transformation of the Chanson at the End of the Fifteenth Century," in *Report of the Tenth Congress of the International Musicological Society, Ljubljana 1967*, ed. Dragotin Cvetko (Kassel: Bärenreiter, 1970), 78–94; and Bernstein, "Notes on the Origin of the Parisian Chanson," *Journal of Musicology* 1 (1982): 275–326.

In addition to providing a distinct subgenre of the chanson, the chanson setting differs in length and often in compositional approach from its sacred counterparts. For instance, temporal manipulations of the borrowed voice that are common to the mass and motet, including the use of augmentation, diminution, and segmentation of the cantus firmus, almost never appear in chanson settings.

3. My category of chanson settings includes what Honey Meconi classifies as cantus firmus settings, as si placet additions, as replacement contratenor versions, and as pieces which "keep two of the original voices but do something other than merely write a new contratenor." Idem, "Art-Song Reworkings: An Overview," *Journal of the Royal Musical Association* 119 (1994): 3–5. The 148 pieces she identifies within the twelve largest families are listed by category on table 1 and as individual works in appendix A in ibid., 4 and 26–36.

4. Many of the families of related settings have been edited. Scholarly editions include *Fors seulement: Thirty Compositions* and *Fortuna desperata: Thirty-Six Settings*. Richard Taruskin produced a series of performance editions: *D'ung aultre amer: Seventeen Settings in Two, Three, Four and Five Parts*, Ogni Sorte Editions, RS 6 (Miami: Ogni Sorte Editions, 1983); *J'ay pris amours: Twenty-Eight Settings in Two, Three, and Four Parts*, Ogni Sorte Editions, RS 5 (Miami: Ogni Sorte Editions, 1982); *L'homme armé: Twenty-One Settings in Two, Three, and Four Parts*, Ogni Sorte Editions, RS 4 (Miami: Ogni Sorte Editions, 1980); and *T'Andernaken: Ten Settings in Three, Four and Five Parts*, Ogni Sorte Editions, RS 7 (Miami: Ogni Sorte Editions, 1981). *De tous biens plaine* is notable for its omission from this list; while numerous individual settings have appeared as part of collected works editions and editions of manuscripts, no broad survey of related settings has appeared. Otto Gombosi's discussion of selected settings in his 1925 monograph, *Jacob Obrecht, eine Stilkritische Studie* (Leipzig: Breitkopf & Härtel, 1925), 34–47, provided the initial foray into this repertory and included a half-dozen transcriptions (ibid., Notenanhang, 24–35). Moreover, the importance of the *De tous biens plaine* family has been acknowledged in the secondary literature for years, and extensive concordance lists detailing related settings have been published by a series of scholars. The most important lists are cited in the critical report. For a study of the sacred music based on *De tous biens plaine*, see Murray Steib, "Loyset Compere and His Recently Rediscovered *Missa De tous biens plaine*," *Journal of Musicology* 11 (1993): 437–54.

5. *De tous biens plaine* was mentioned in two morality plays and cited in three of Jean Molinet's poems. It was also used as a motto. See Brown, *Music in the French Secular Theater, 1400–1550* (Cambridge, MA: Harvard University Press, 1963), 204–6.

6. Abbreviations for manuscript and print sources are used here and following. Complete library information and call numbers for these sources are given in the critical report.

7. See, for example, *The New Grove Dictionary of Music and Musicians*, s.v. "Hayne van Ghizeghem," by Louise Litterick.

8. The four traditional Franco-Burgundian sources from the 1460s and 1470s that contain Hayne's setting include Laborde, Wolfenbüttel, Dijon, and Cop 291/8. Other early sources include Pavia 362 and Cordiforme from Savoy, and Mellon and Sev/P from Naples. The 1480s and 1490s saw further copies from France (Ricc 2794 and Uppsala 76a) and Naples (Bologna Q16, Monte Cassino, and Perugia 431) as well as copies in the Florentine sources (Pixérécourt, Ricc 2356, Flor 178, and CG) and the Ferrarese chansonnier Casanatense. A complete listing of concordances for Hayne's setting can be found in the critical commentary for setting 1.

9. Sacred redactions of Hayne's chanson fall somewhat earlier than the chanson settings, for Compere's motet *Omnium bonorum plenum* and several of the mass settings appear to date from the 1470s and 1480s. The chanson settings, then, may reflect a "second wave" in the song's popularity which began in the 1490s and extended over the next two decades.

Although somewhat slower to flourish as a model for secular settings than some of the other popular chansons of the period—Meconi has shown that *J'ay pris amours*, *D'ung aultre amer*, and *Fortuna desperata* all began spawning settings in the 1470s; see idem, "Art-Song Reworkings," 7, table 2—Hayne's chanson ultimately inspired a greater number of reworkings than any of its contemporaneous musical models, resulting in six masses, four mass sections, four motets, four combinative or quodlibet settings, five bicinia, three settings which survive as fragments, and the twenty-eight settings provided here.

10. Published arrangements issued by Petrucci include two settings in the *Odhecaton* of 1501 (settings 8 and 19); one each in *Canti B* (setting 11) and *Motetti A* (setting 10), both issued in 1502; and six in *Canti C* (settings 6, 12, 14, 16, 17a, and 27), which was published in 1504.

11. England is represented by a copy of Hayne's setting in London 31922, known as "Henry VIII Manuscript"; the chanson's late circulation in Germany is reflected both by Ulm 237 and by the lone surviving discant partbook published by Egenolff and now housed as Paris, Bibliothèque Nationale, Rés. Vm^7 504. Similarly, the Nuremburg publications by Formschneider (1538) and Newsidler (1536) contain, respectively, a copy of setting 16 and a lute intabulation of the Ghiselin setting found here as setting 11.

12. Most of the sources containing arrangements stem from the 1490s and early 1500s, giving a *terminus ante quem* to the repertory. A few later sources also provide arrangements: Mun 239 from the mid-1510s contains a work by Josquin (setting 8), and the late German sources Newsidler, from 1536, and Formschneider, from 1538, contain copies of a work by Ghiselin (setting 11) and an anonymous tenor-based arrangement (setting 16) respectively, but all three

settings are demonstrably earlier, for all were issued by Petrucci in the first few years of the century. Only setting 28 by D'Oude Scheure is chronologically and stylistically removed from the rest of the complex: its partbook source, Cambrai 125–28, comes from 1542, and the setting itself is unlike any other, transposing the tenor to A and employing significant variants. Dates for all manuscript and print sources are provided in the critical report.

13. Ghiselin also spent some time working alongside Alexander Agricola at Naples in 1494. See Allan W. Atlas and Anthony M. Cummings, "Agricola, Ghiselin, and Alfonso II of Naples," *Journal of Musicology* 7 (1989): 540–48.

14. Agricola's repertory, though predominantly found in Italian musical sources such as the Petrucci prints, CG, and Verona 757, also makes its way into Flor C 2439, the so-called Basevi Codex, from the Low Countries. Josquin's offerings appear in the Swiss sources Mun 239 and Glareanus as well as in Petrucci's *Odhecaton* and his *Motetti A*.

15. De Planquard's setting 7 survives in the Florentine source Banco Rari 229; Bactio's setting 24 is found in Bologna Q17; D'Oude Schuere's setting 28 appears in Cambrai 125–28.

16. The idea of a composer's one-upsmanship reflects Brown's evocation of competition as a motivation for a model-based repertory in his seminal article, "Emulation, Competition, and Homage: Imitation and Theories of Imitation in the Renaissance," *Journal of the American Musicological Society* 35 (1982): 1–48. As Brown remarks, "we shall never know whether such emulation or imitation was practiced to compete with other composers—to demonstrate superior expertise using the same musical materials—or to pay them homage. In truth the two impulses are doubtless closely related." Ibid., 10. If the motivations of the composers are uncertain, the experience of the reading audience was certainly shaped by the scribe's awareness of connections between one setting and another. Certain chansonniers provide groups of related settings as if creating a mini-anthology to facilitate direct comparison of the arrangements. The compiler of Flor C 2439, for instance, collects as many as seven compositions based on the same polyphonic model.

17. In the *J'ay pris amours* family, for instance, contrapuntal manipulations abound. Japart's canonic setting (see Brown, *Music in the French Secular Theater*, setting p) involves transposing the superius down a twelfth and performing it in retrograde. Busnois (ibid., setting bb) inverts and varies the superius, and Isaac (ibid., setting r) develops a newly composed, motivically obsessive contratenor part that repeats the superius's motto more than twenty times over the course of the piece.

18. Brown, "Emulation," 47–48. As Brown points out earlier in his article, the additive technique of setting a cantus firmus into a new polyphonic context was not new in the fifteenth century; see ibid., 10–11. In his discussion, Brown mentions settings 5 and 7 in passing as examples of substituting a faster contratenor or a closely-spaced canonic pair of voices for an original contratenor line. He argues that this "is simply an adaptation of the cantus-firmus principle, in which the composer glosses an older original in order to transform it, in these cases, into a presumably instrumental arrangement of an old favorite." Ibid., 11.

19. The practice of adding si placet parts has been examined extensively in Stephen Self, "The 'Si Placet' Voice: An Historical and Analytical Study" (Ph.D. diss., Ohio State University, 1990). Some of that material also appears in *The Si Placet Repertoire of 1480–1530*, ed. Stephen Self, Recent Researches in the Music of the Renaissance, vol. 106 (Madison: A-R Editions, 1996).

20. Although the *Odhecaton* version has circulated under Hayne's name in the secondary literature, the reading is transmitted anonymously. Since all of Hayne's other chansons with the exception of *A la audienche* are *a 3*, it is unlikely that the *Odhecaton* altus is by Hayne himself.

21. The principal study of Japart's chanson style can be found in Ralph Buxton, "Johannes Japart: A Fifteenth-Century Chanson Composer," *Current Musicology* 31 (1981): 7–38. His focus is largely on the combinative offerings, which are by their nature texturally complicated. The preponderance of Japart's repertory adopts the imitative style of the four-part popular arrangements as characterized by Brown, "Genesis of a Style," 24–25, in which the chanson rustique (or perhaps a newly composed popular tune) informs the polyphony of at least two and usually all four voices.

Perhaps the best parallel to the canon for setting 27 can be found with his setting of *J'ay pris amours* from *Canti B* and elsewhere. The canon is given variously as "Fit aries piscis in licanos ypathon" (*Canti B*), "Antiphrasis baritonat" (in the Florentine sources Banco Rari 229, fols. 158v–159 and Flor 178, fols. 4v–5), and "Vade retro sathanas" (in CG). Helen Hewitt has eloquently explained the references to the zodiac and to Greek nomenclature in *Canti B*, showing that the canon found there suggests the necessary retrograde motion, and explicitly instructs the performer to start "a twelfth below the opening tone, a', of the borrowed *cantus firmus*." *Canti B, Numero Cinquanta, Venice, 1502*, ed. Helen Hewitt, Monuments of Renaissance Music, vol. 2 (Chicago and London: University of Chicago Press, 1967), 63. The less explicit "antiphrasis baritonat" and "vade retro sathanas" both have an element of playfulness, for the performer must decipher the canon, presumably through trial and error. For a discussion of the *Canti B* canon and for concordances to the *J'ay pris amours* setting, see ibid.

22. The term *redictae* comes from Tinctoris, *Liber de arte contrapuncti*, Liber Tertius, capitulum VI, "De sexta generali regula que redictas fieri prohibet"; see Johannes Tinctoris, *Opera theoretica*, ed. Albert Seay, Corpus scriptorum de musica, vol. 22 (N.p.: American Institute of Musicology, 1975), 152–54. As Tinctoris explains, "redictas nihil aliud est quam unius aut plurium conjunctionum continua repetitio" (repetition is nothing other than the continuous reiteration of one or many motives). Ibid., 154. None of the examples Tinctoris supplies in the chapter, however, offers a systematic application of the technique.

In addition to deciphering the tenor's abbreviations for setting 9, Allan Atlas also determined that the opening in question contains two discrete settings which share a superius part. The borrowed superius melody is shared by a tenor-contratenor pair that give Hayne's original chanson (setting 1) and by a second tenor-contratenor pair that are unique to setting 9. This solution avoids the dissonances of previous five-voice editions of the piece. See Atlas, *The Cappella Giulia Chansonnier: Rome, Biblioteca Apostolica Vaticana, C.G.XIII.27*, Musicological Studies, vol. 27 (Brooklyn: Institute of Mediaeval Music, 1976), 1:137–39.

23. Some damage to the source has in fact resulted from someone's attempts to separate the two pages.

24. Richard Wexler, "Newly Identified Works by Bartolomeo degli Organi in the MS Bologna Q17," *Journal of the American Musicological Society* 23 (1970): 107–18.

25. Certain other infelicitous reworkings—for instance, settings 5, 18, and 26 in this edition—may also reflect the

inexpert hand of the student composer, for awkward phrase junctions, irregular resolutions of dissonances, and disjointed melodic contours mar the contrapuntal fabric of these works. The substitute-contratenor version of setting 4 is especially weak, as is discussed in its commentary. Nevertheless, caution should prevail in evaluating such settings, for slap-dash compositional decisions may reflect the relatively transitory nature of a repertory intended more for entertainment than for aesthetic investigation. The methodology successfully employed by both Wexler and Brown to establish the pedagogical function of specific works in this repertory points out musical parallels between model and reworking that go beyond a compositional relationship that is simply informed by a cantus firmus treatment. It is significant that Brown's primary examples of student works are not, in fact, cantus firmus settings at all; see Brown, "Emulation," 2–8 and 12–13.

26. Linz is a set of manuscript fragments which lack foliation. They had been used as binding material, and were both cropped and mutilated. A film of the fragments is available at the Hill Monastic Manuscript Library, where historian Eric Reiter drew my attention to it. The piece under discussion here would be 8v according to the microfilmed order, but the leaves have been reorganized in the Linz collection.

27. This setting was first identified by Martin Staehelin, who provides a discussion and full facsimile of the Augsburg source; see "Das Augsburger Fragment: Eine wenig beachtete süddeutsche Quelle zur mehrstimmingen Musik des späten 15. und des frühen 16. Jahrhunderts," *Augsburger Jahrbuch für Musikwissenschaft* 4 (1987): 7–63; the facsimile of *De tous biens plaine* is found on page 41.

28. The issue of "voices versus instruments" has been a hotly contested one. Although in the 1970s scholars assumed that an absence of text necessarily meant instrumental performance, the so-called English a cappella heresy led by Christopher Page and David Fallows has pointed to the remarkable lack of documentation for combinations of voices and instruments. See, for instance, Page, "The Performance of Songs in Late Medieval France: A New Source," *Early Music* 10 (1982): 441–50; Fallows, "Specific Information on the Ensembles for Composed Polyphony, 1400–1474," in *Studies in the Performance of Late Mediaeval Music*, ed. Stanley Boorman (New York: Cambridge University Press, 1983), 109–59; and idem, "Secular Polyphony in the Fifteenth Century," in *Performance Practice*, vol. 1, *Music Before 1600*, ed. Howard Mayer Brown and Stanley Sadie, The Norton/Grove Handbooks in Music (New York: W. W. Norton, 1990), 201–21, esp. 203–9. Moreover, Lloyd Hibberd has noted that many of the elements claimed as characteristically instrumental show up in contemporaneous mass movements; see Hibberd, "On 'Instrumental Style' in Early Melody," *Musical Quarterly* 32 (1946): 107–30. Voices alone likely remained one of several performance options for the chanson until the rise of the Parisian chanson in the 1520s again made a cappella singing the predominant texture.

For this transitional period, Louise Litterick has offered a nuanced view of the manuscript tradition, noting that a decline in the provision of texted parts within the manuscript tradition in Italy during the later fifteenth century might reflect a break from the northern texted performance practice. See Litterick, "Performing Franco-Netherlandish Secular Music of the Late Fifteenth Century: Texted and Untexted Parts in the Sources," *Early Music* 8 (1980): 474–85; idem, "On Italian Instrumental Ensemble Music in the Late Fifteenth Century," in *Music in Medieval and Early Modern Europe: Patronage, Sources and Texts*, ed. Iain Fenlon (Cambridge and New York: Cambridge University Press, 1981), 117–30. That instrumentalists were in a position to use the kind of repertory found in chansonniers is apparent both from the rise in musical literacy, as documented by anecdotal accounts (including that of Benvenuto Cellini!), and by the references to musical sources intended for instrumentalists, most notably the *Cantiones a la pifarescha* in the Casanatense chansonnier.

Most scholars now believe that pragmatic considerations—who was available—likely determined the choice of timbre for the late-fifteenth- and early-sixteenth-century chanson (particularly by 1475, when instrumental ensembles seem to shift their functions, supplementing improvisatory practice by more frequent recourse to the written repertory). See, for instance, the brief survey of performance options in Brown, "On the Performance of Fifteenth-Century Chansons," *Early Music* 1 (1973): 3–10.

29. In general, those settings preserving the discant-tenor framework (i.e. settings 1–6) also maintain the medial cadence, while those drawing a single voice from the model do not, though exceptions can be found. Of the superius-based settings, 12 and 14 retain the medial cadence, and 14 even includes a *signum congruentiae* to mark the spot. Of the tenor-based settings, only 17a, 19, and 26 provide a clear-cut medial resting point. In the remaining settings, a variety of techniques serve to disguise the former medial arrival, including, but not limited to, rhythmic and motivic devices, elided and staggered phrase endings, and harmonic recomposition.

Text and Translation

De tous biens plaine est ma maistresse,
Chacun lui doit tribut d'onneur.
Car assouvye est en valeur
Autant que jamais fut deesse.

En la veant j'ay tel leesse
Que c'est paradis en mon cuer.
De tous biens plaine est ma maistresse,
Chacun lui doit tribut d'onneur.

Je n'ay cure d'autre richesse
Si non d'estre son serviteur,
Et pource qu'il n'est choix milleur
En mon mot porteray sans cesse:

De tous biens plaine est ma maistresse,
Chacun lui doit tribut d'onneur.
Car assouvye est en valeur
Autant que jamais fut deesse.

   Source. Laborde, fol. 62v.

My mistress is full of all good virtue,
Everyone owes her honorable tribute.
For she is accomplished in merit
As much as a goddess ever was.

When I see her I have such cheer
That paradise is in my heart.
My mistress is full of all good virtue,
Everyone owes her honorable tribute.

I have no care for other riches
Except to be her servant,
And because there is no better choice,
I carry as my unceasing motto:

My mistress is full of all good virtue,
Everyone owes her honorable tribute.
For she is accomplished in merit
As much as a goddess ever was.

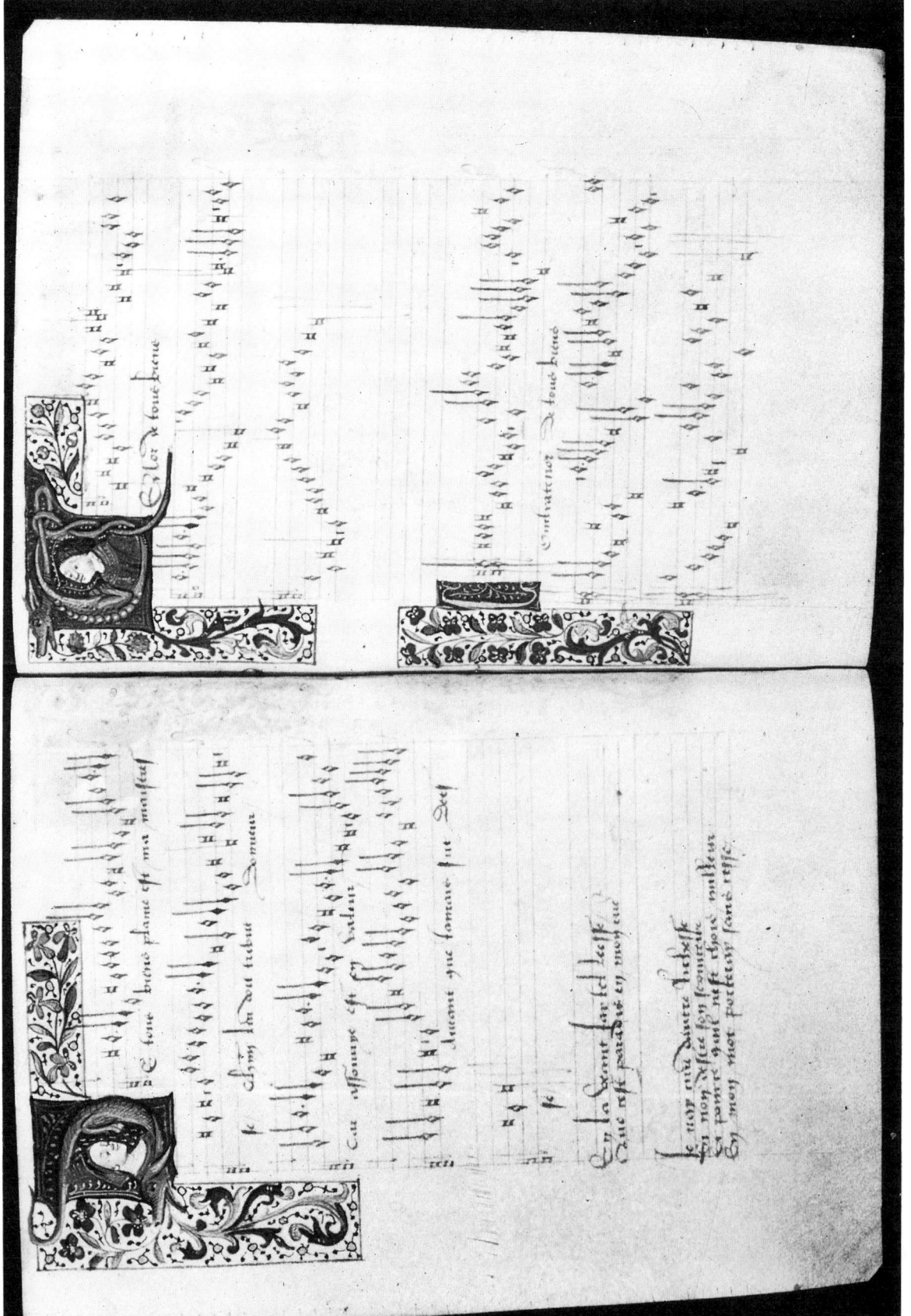

Plate 1. Hayne van Ghizeghem, *De tous biens plaine* (setting 1), superius, tenor, and contratenor. Washington, Library of Congress, Music Division, MS M.2.1.L25 Case ("Laborde Chansonnier"), fols. 62v–63r. Reproduced by permission from the Music Division of the Library of Congress.

Twenty-Eight Settings of
De tous biens plaine

The Original Version
1. De tous biens plaine

Laborde, fols. 62v–63r [Hayne van Ghizeghem]

Si Placet Settings

2. De tous biens playne

Odhecaton, no. 20, fols. 22v–23r
Anonymous

3. [De tous biens plaine]

Bologna Q18, fol. 48r

Anonymous

Substitute Contratenor Settings
4. De tous biens playne

Flor Panc 27, no. 36, fol. 25r Anonymous

17

5. De tous biens plaine

Banco Rari 229, fols. 187v–188r [no. 177]

Anonymous

21
ne[u]r.
26
Car
Car
31
as- sou- - - vi- - e'est en
as- - sou- vi- - e'est
37
va- - - leur
en va- leur

19

6. De tous biens

Canti C, no. 118, fols. 143v–144r

Anonymous

-neur.
-but d'on- - neur.
Car
Car as- - sou-
Car as- - sou- vy-
-vy- e est en va- leur
- e'est en va- - -

41
Au- tant que ja-
-leur Au- tant que ja-
46
- mais, [au- tant que
- mais, [au- tant
51
ja- - mais] fut de-
que ja- mais] fut de- es-
56
-es- - - - se.
- - - - se.

7. De tous bien

Banco Rari 229, fols. 188v–189r [no. 178]
de Planquard

[Superius]

[T]enor — [D]E tous bien / De tous bien

[Contratenor 1] — De tous bien

[Contratenor 2] — [De tous bien]

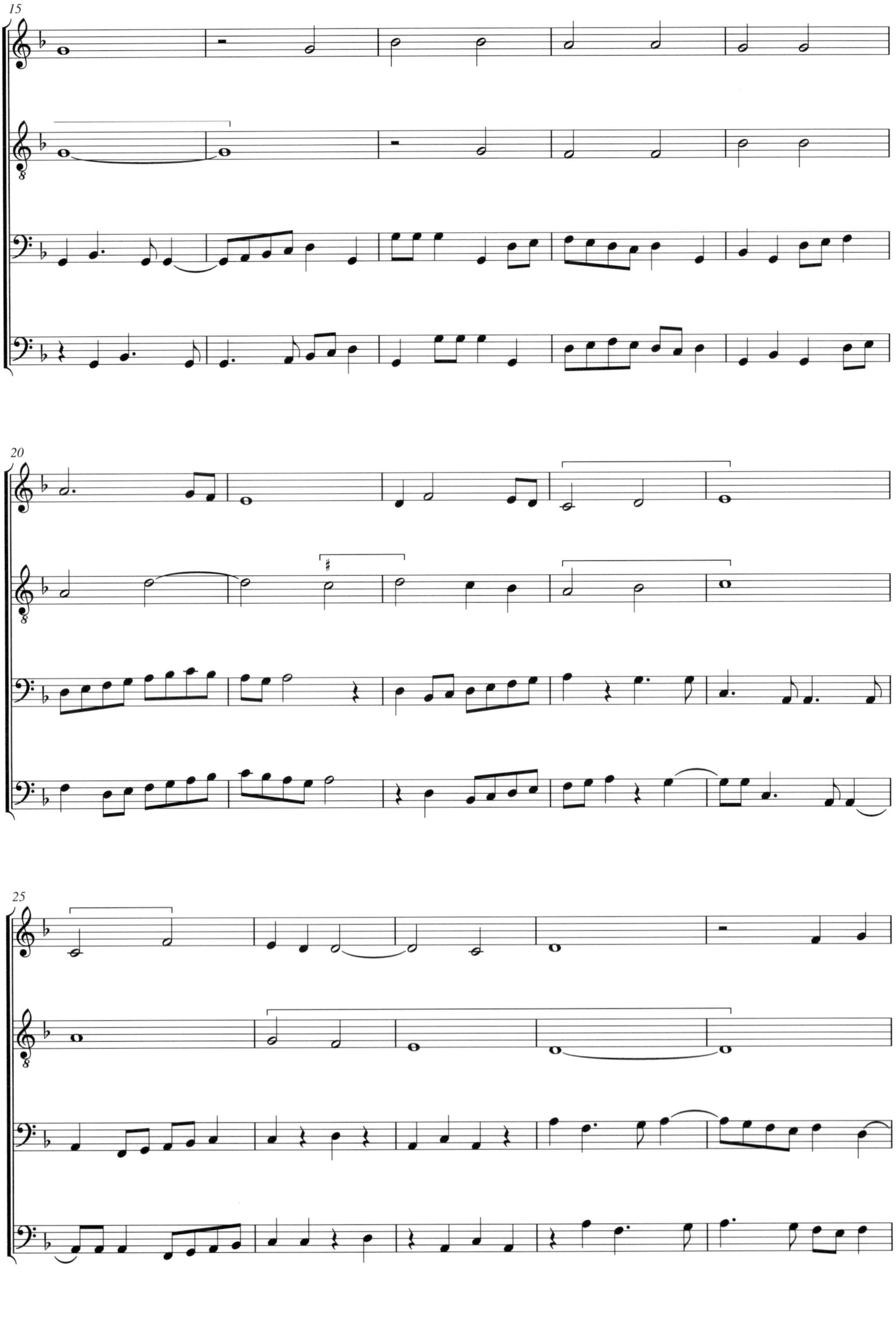
15
20
25

25

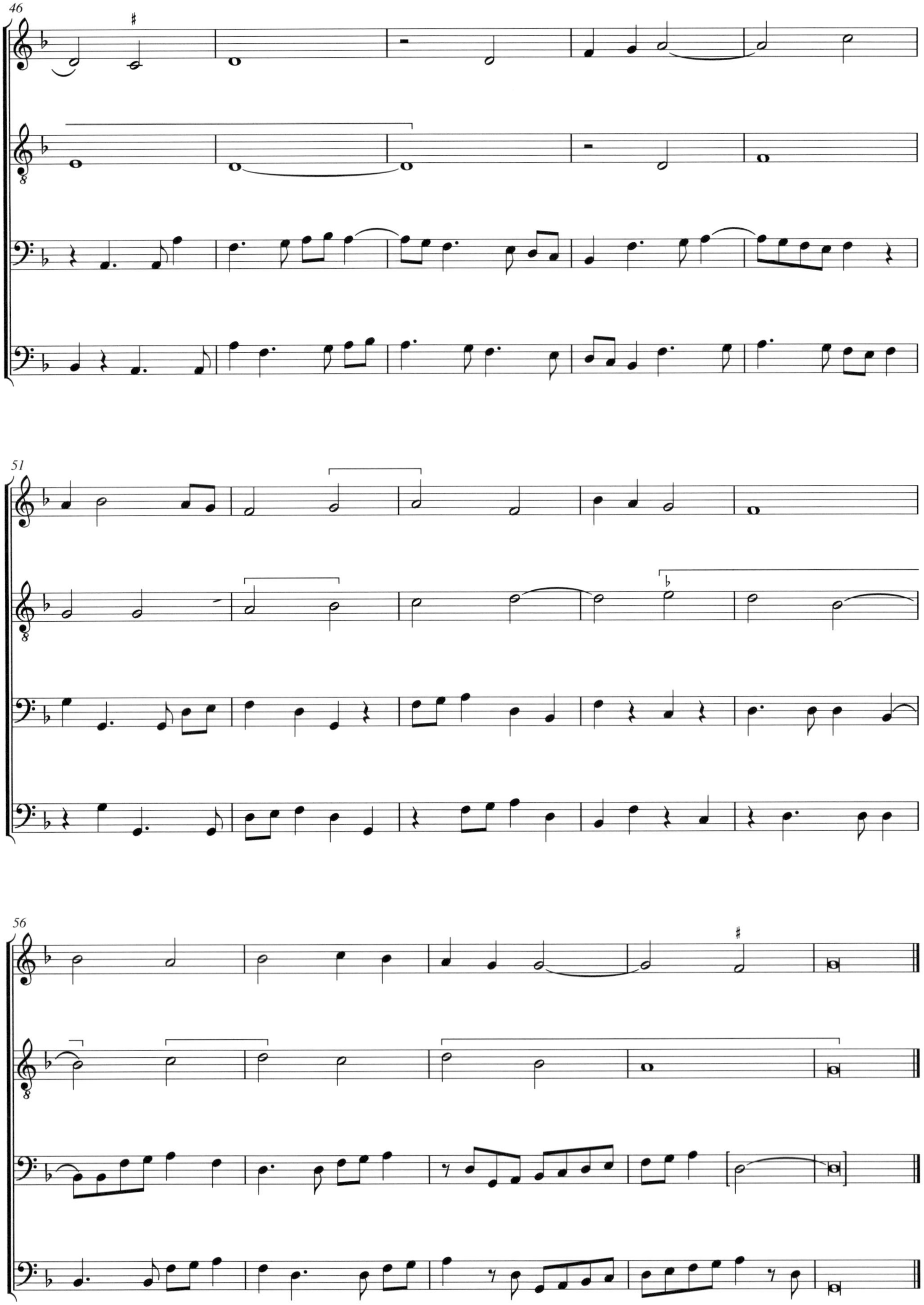
46
51
56

8. [De tous biens plaine]

Mun 239, fols. 15v–16r

[Josquin des Prez]

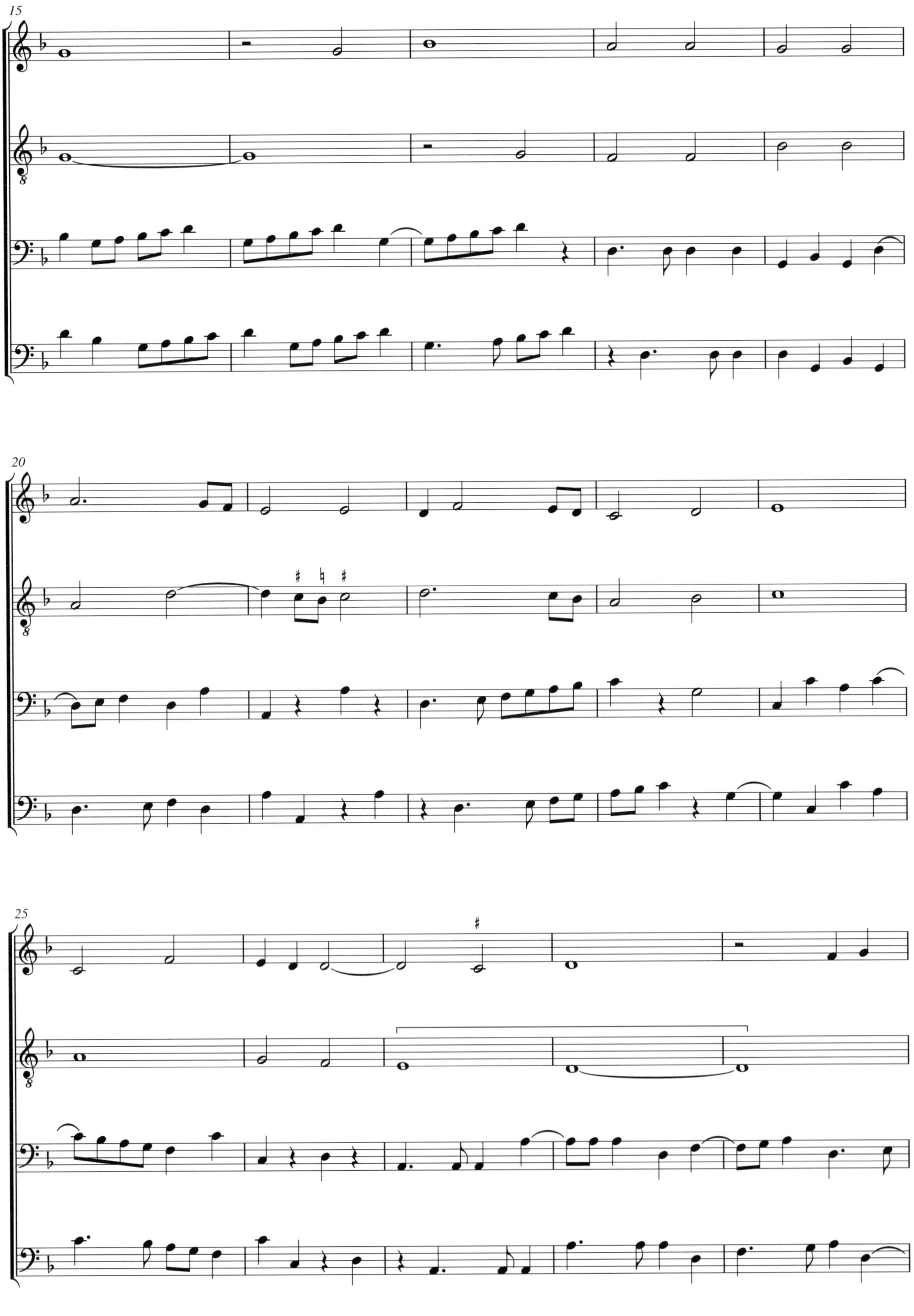
15
20
25

29

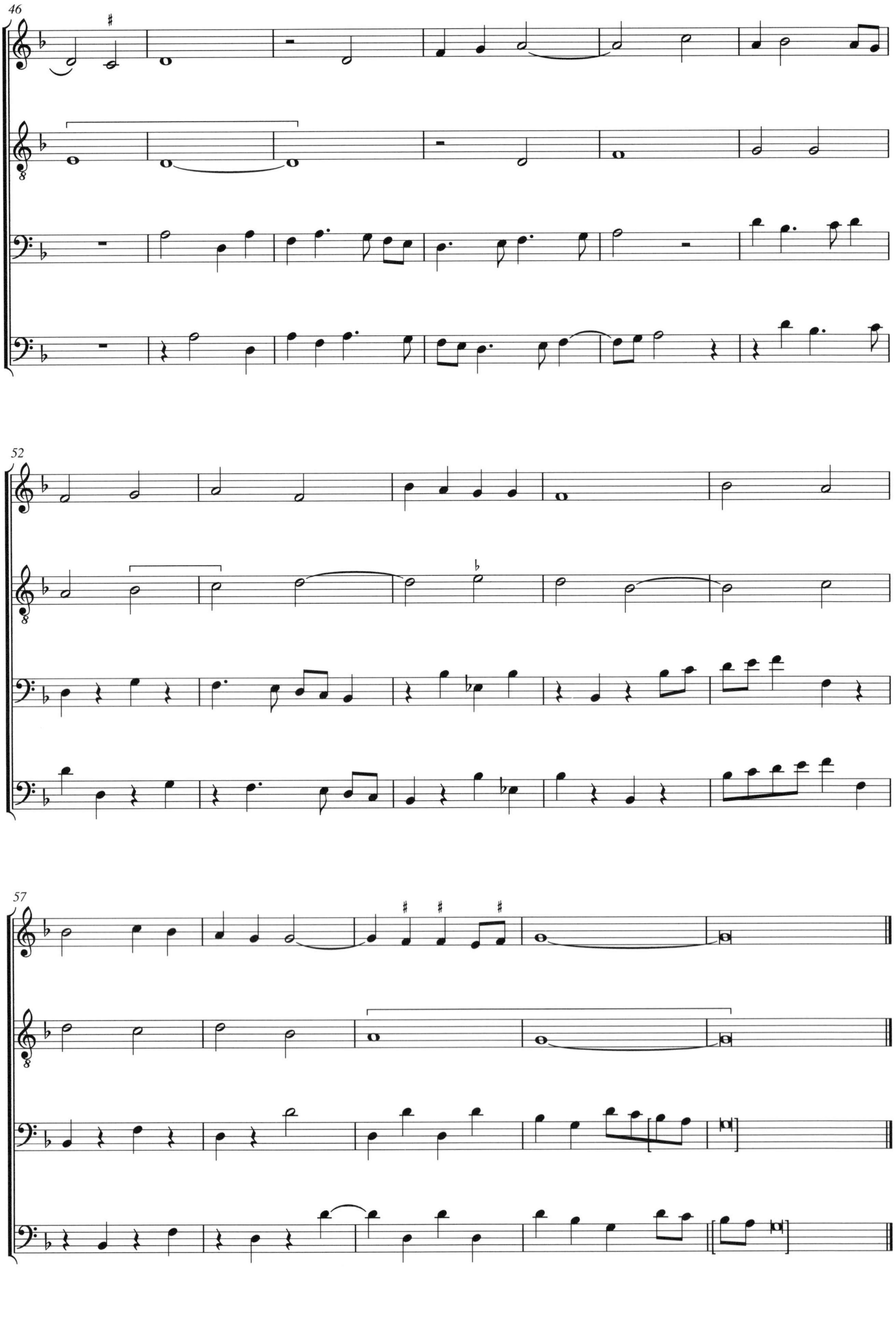
46
52
57

Settings Based on the Superius
9. De tobiens plena

CG, fols. 57v–58r (64v–65r)　　　　　　　　　　　　　　　　　　　　　　　　　　　　　　　Anonymous

[Superius]

Tenor

Bassus

De tobiens plena

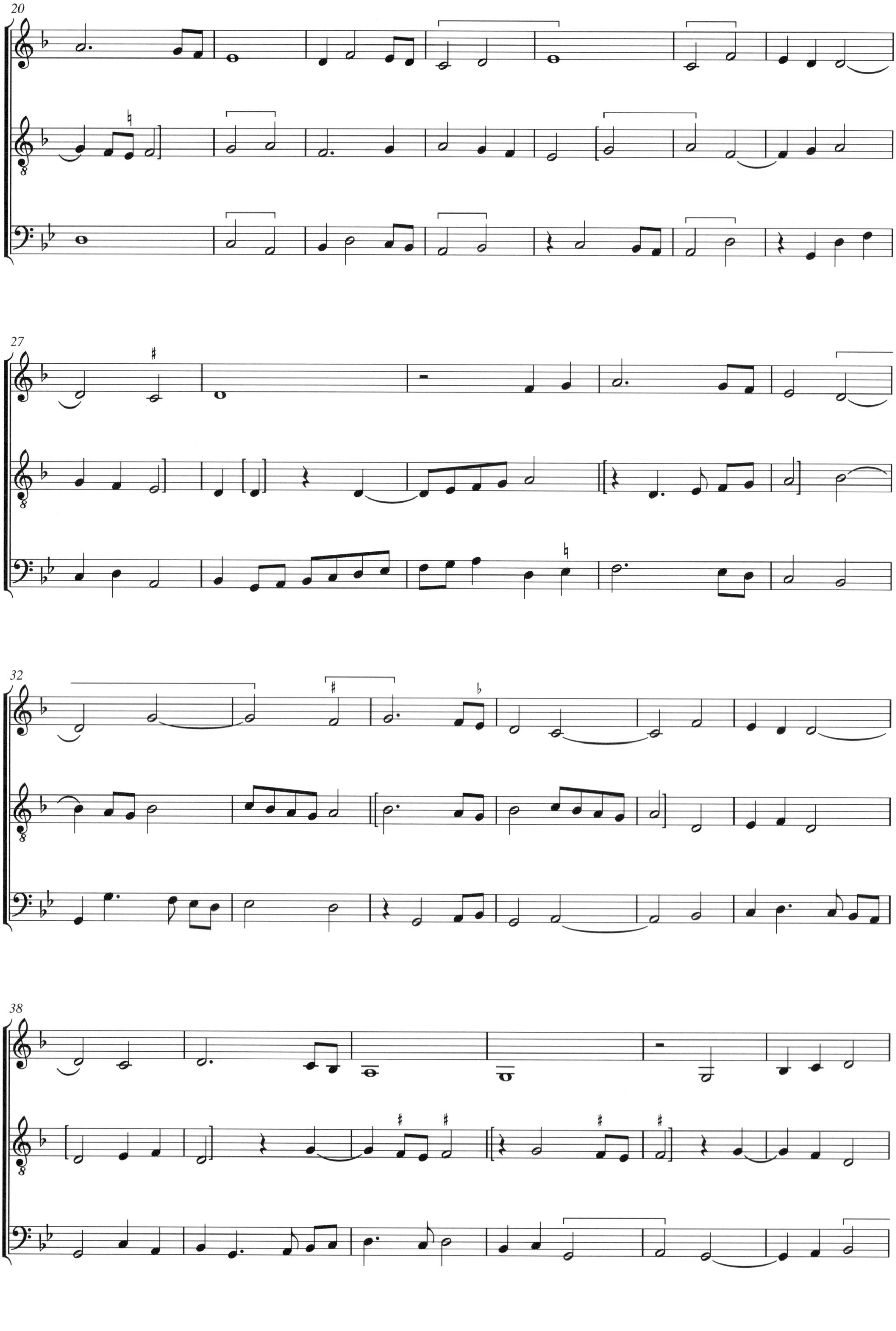
20
27
32
38

33

10. De tous biens

Motetti A, fol. 55v

Josquin [des Prez]

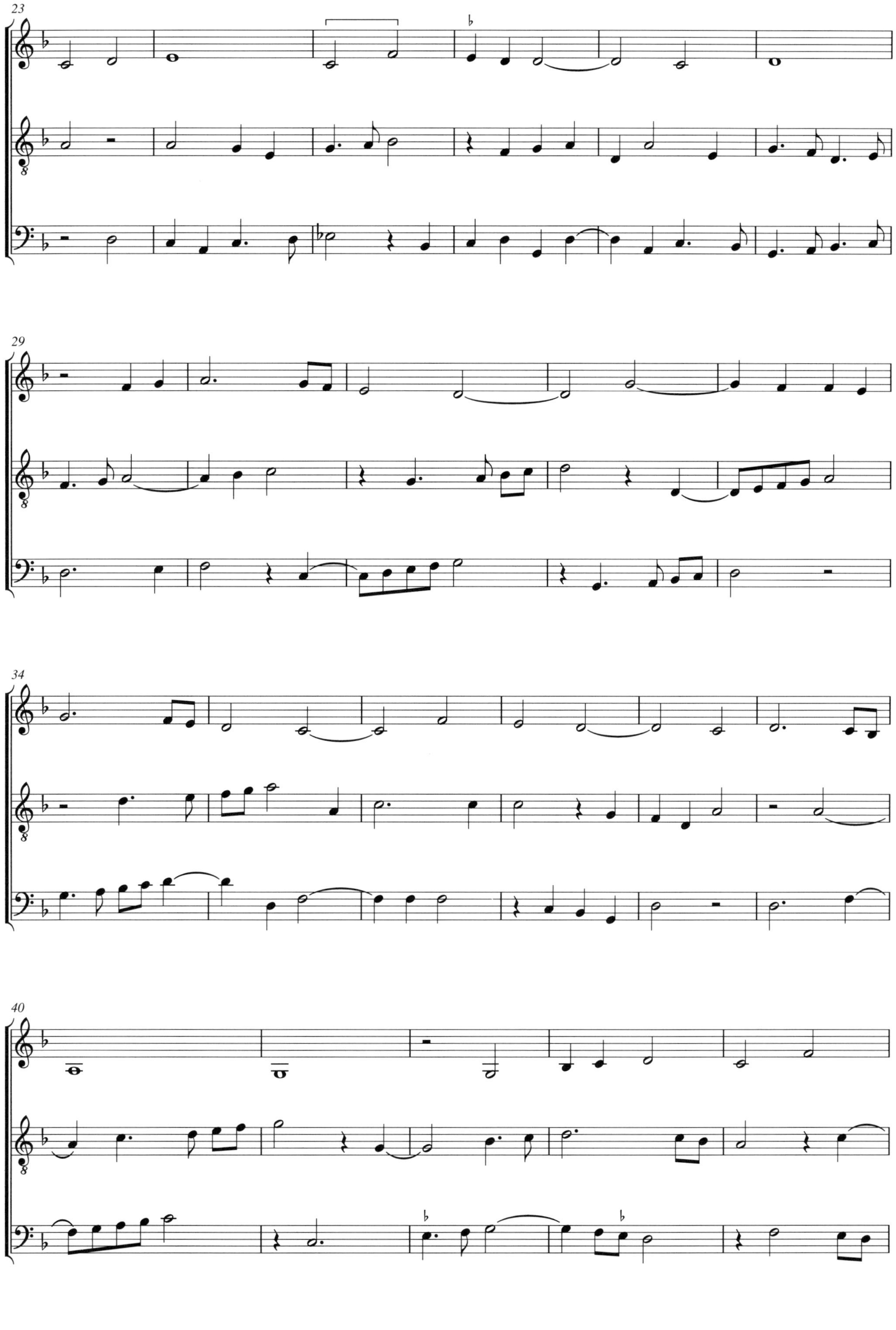
23
29
34
40

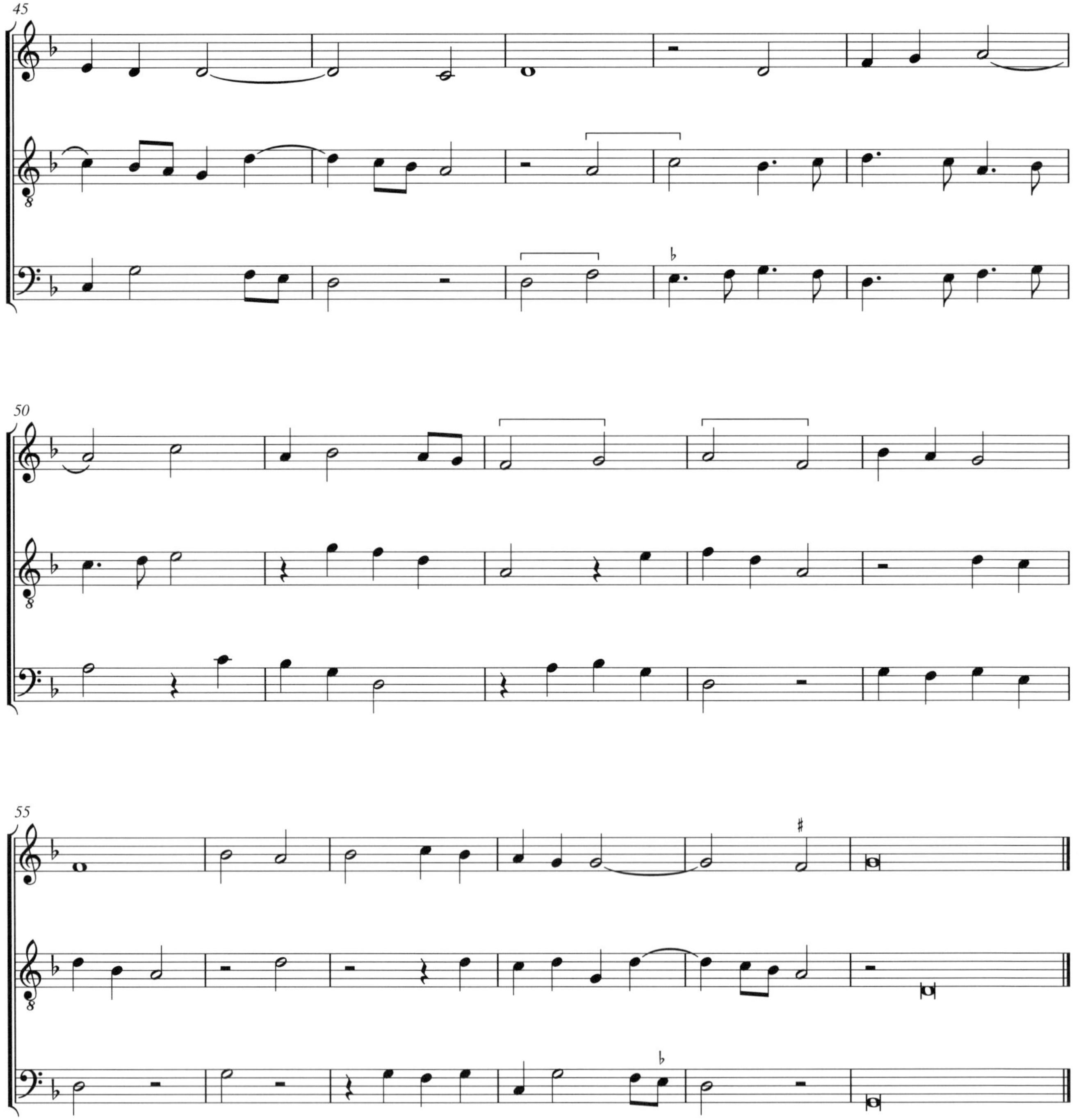

11. De tous biens

Canti B, no. 42, fols. 45v–46r

[Johannes] Ghiselin [*dit* Verbonnet]

[Superius]

DE tous biens

Tenor

Contra

De tous biens

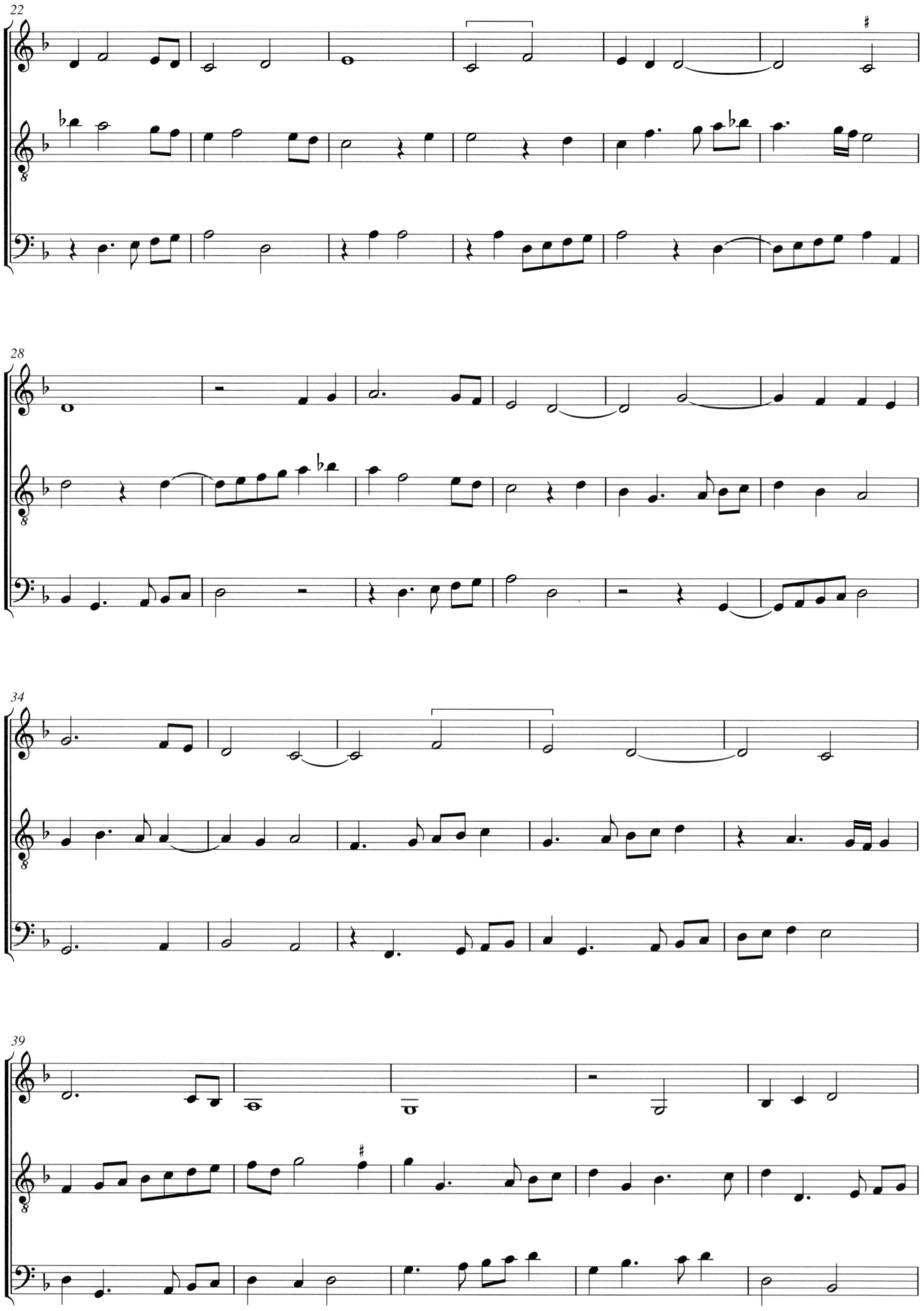
22
28
34
39

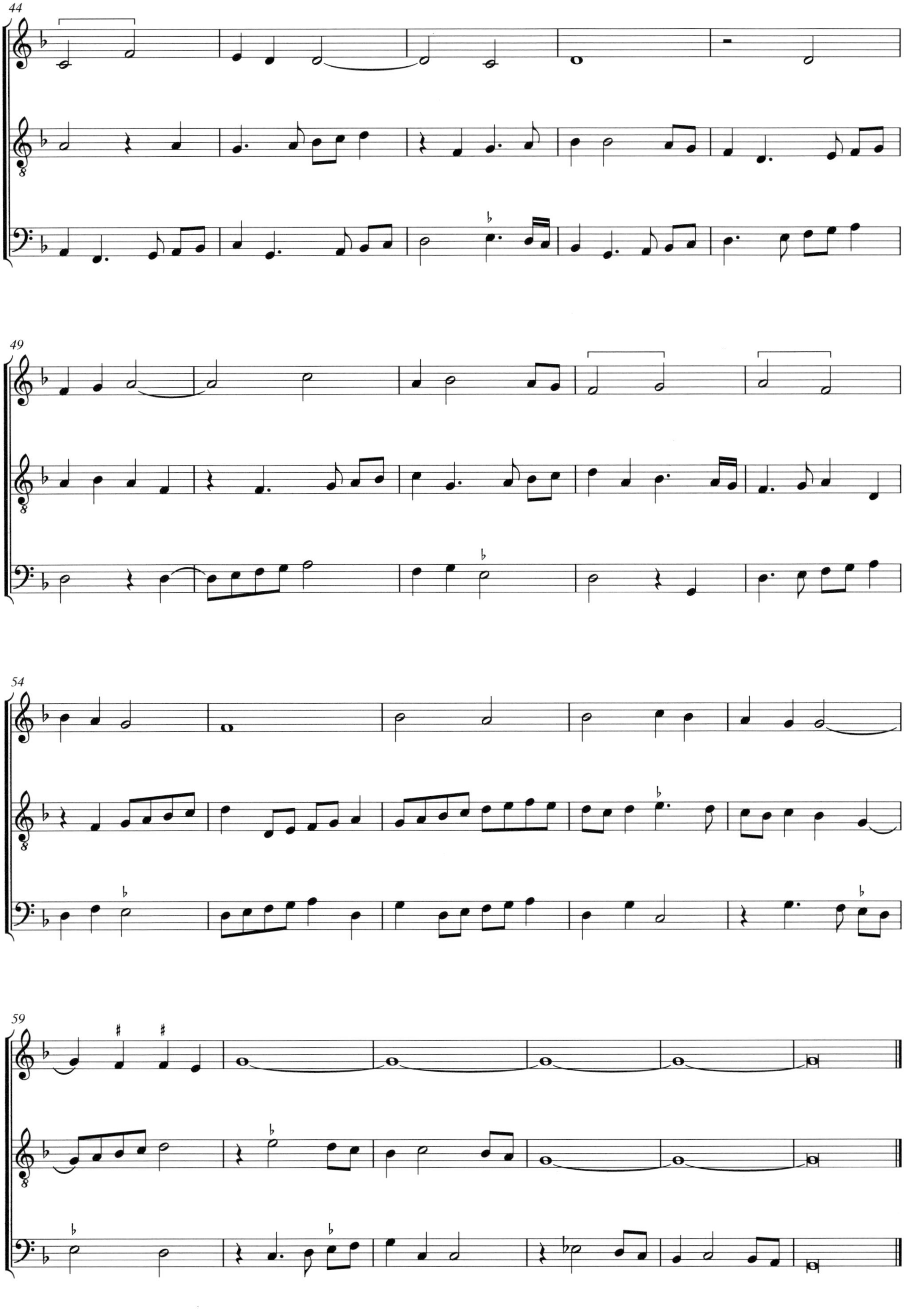
44
49
54
59

12. De tous biens playne

Canti C, no. 66, fols. 88v–89r

Anonymous

-se, Cha- cun lui doit tri- but d'on- neur.

Car as-

- sou- vy- e est en va- leur Autant que ja- - mais, [au-

-tant que ja - mais] fut

de- es - - - se.

13. [De tous biens plaine]

Mun 3154, no. 31, fols. 49v–50r

Anonymous

45

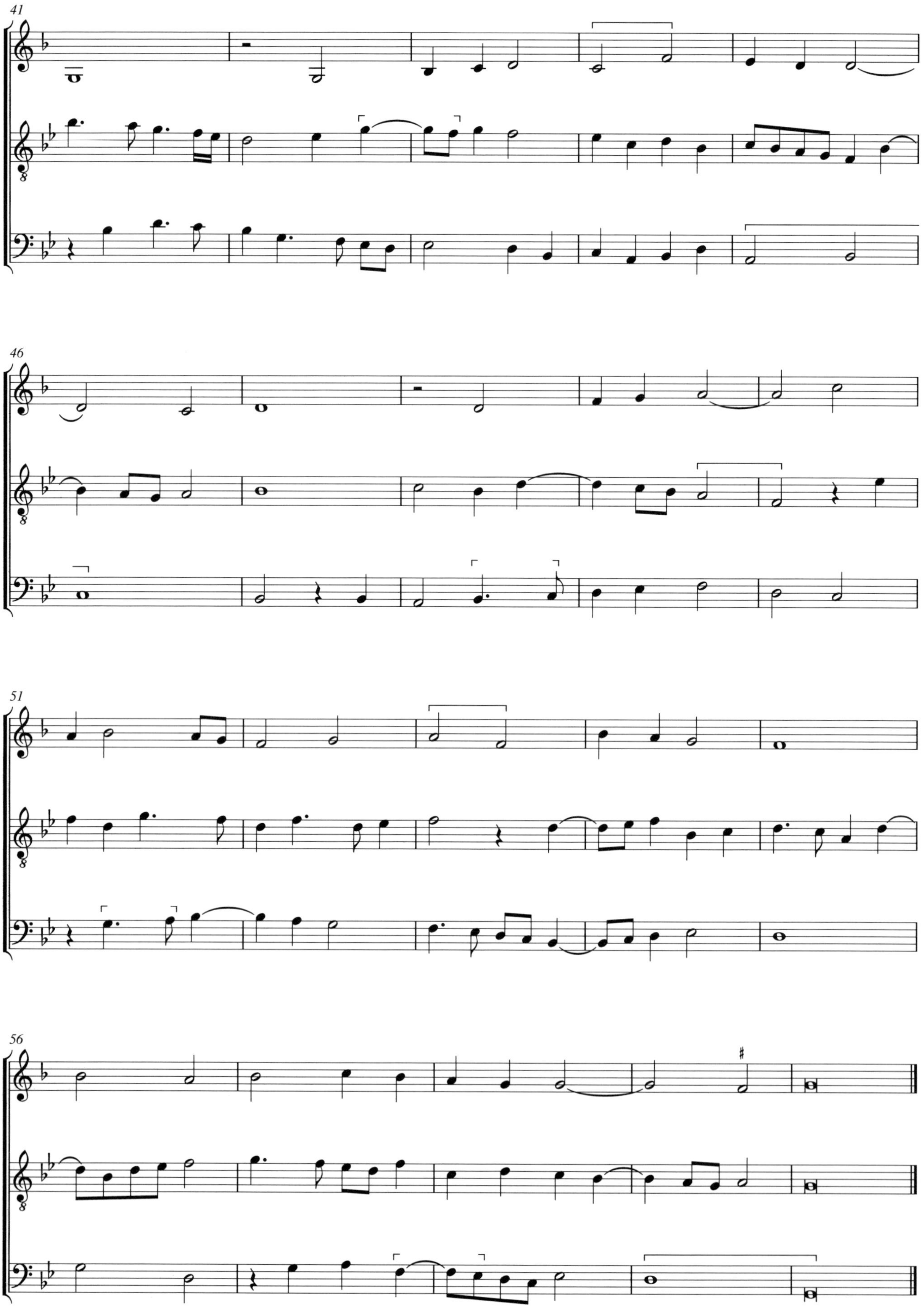
41
46
51
56

14. De tous biens

Canti C, no. 84, fols. 110v–111r

Anonymous

Cha- cun lui doit tri- but d'on- neur.

Car

as- sou- vy- e

est en va- leur

Au- tant que jamais, [au- tant que ja- - mais] fut de- -es- - - - se.

Settings Based on the Tenor
15. [De tous biens plaine]

Verona 757, fols. 43v–44r

Anonymous

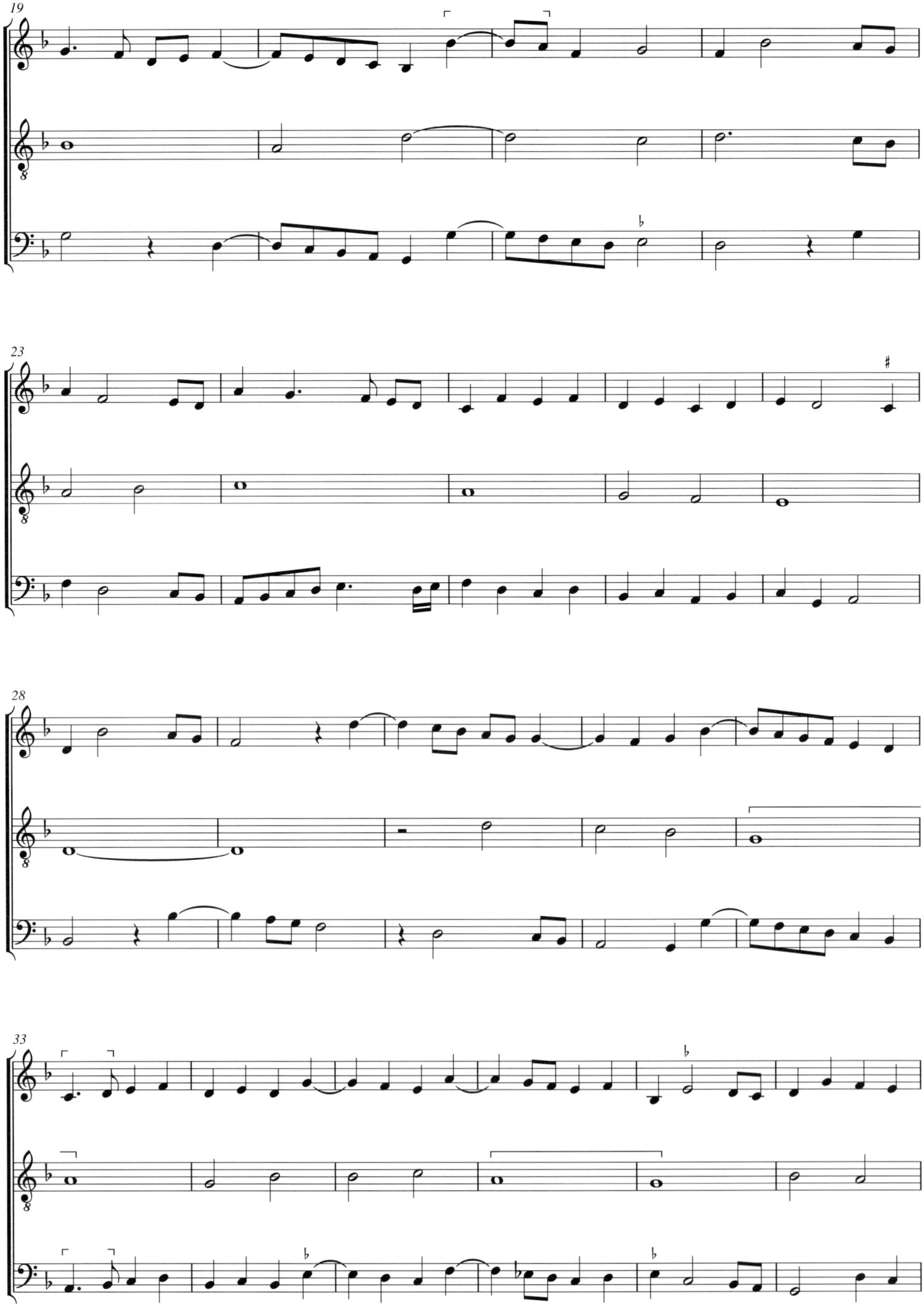
19
23
28
33

53

16. De tobiens plaine e ma maetressa

CG, fols. 17v–18r (24v–25r)

Anonymous

DE tobiens plaine e ma maetressa

55

56

17a. De tous biens

Canti C, no. 62, fols. 83v–84r

[Alexander] Agricola

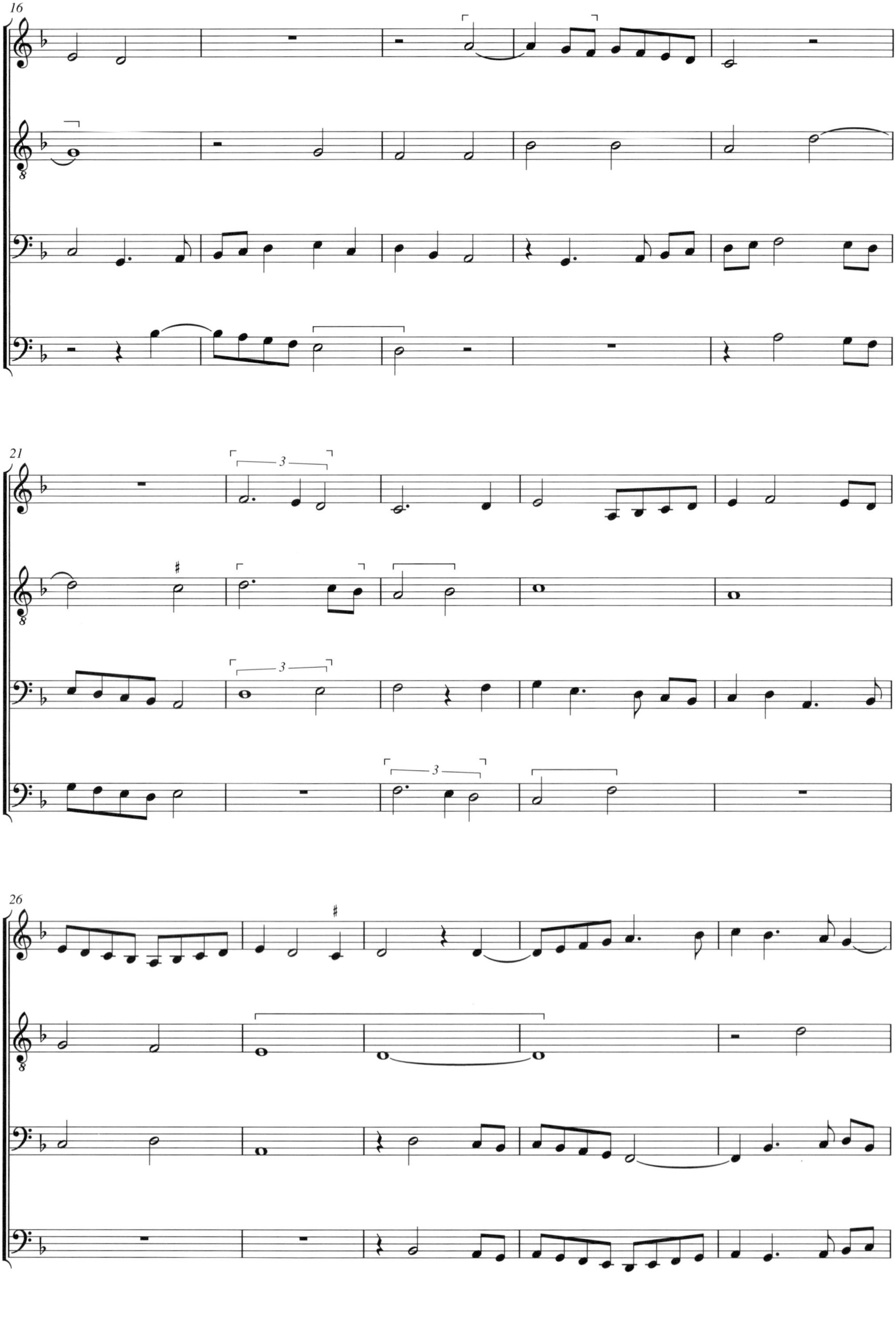

59

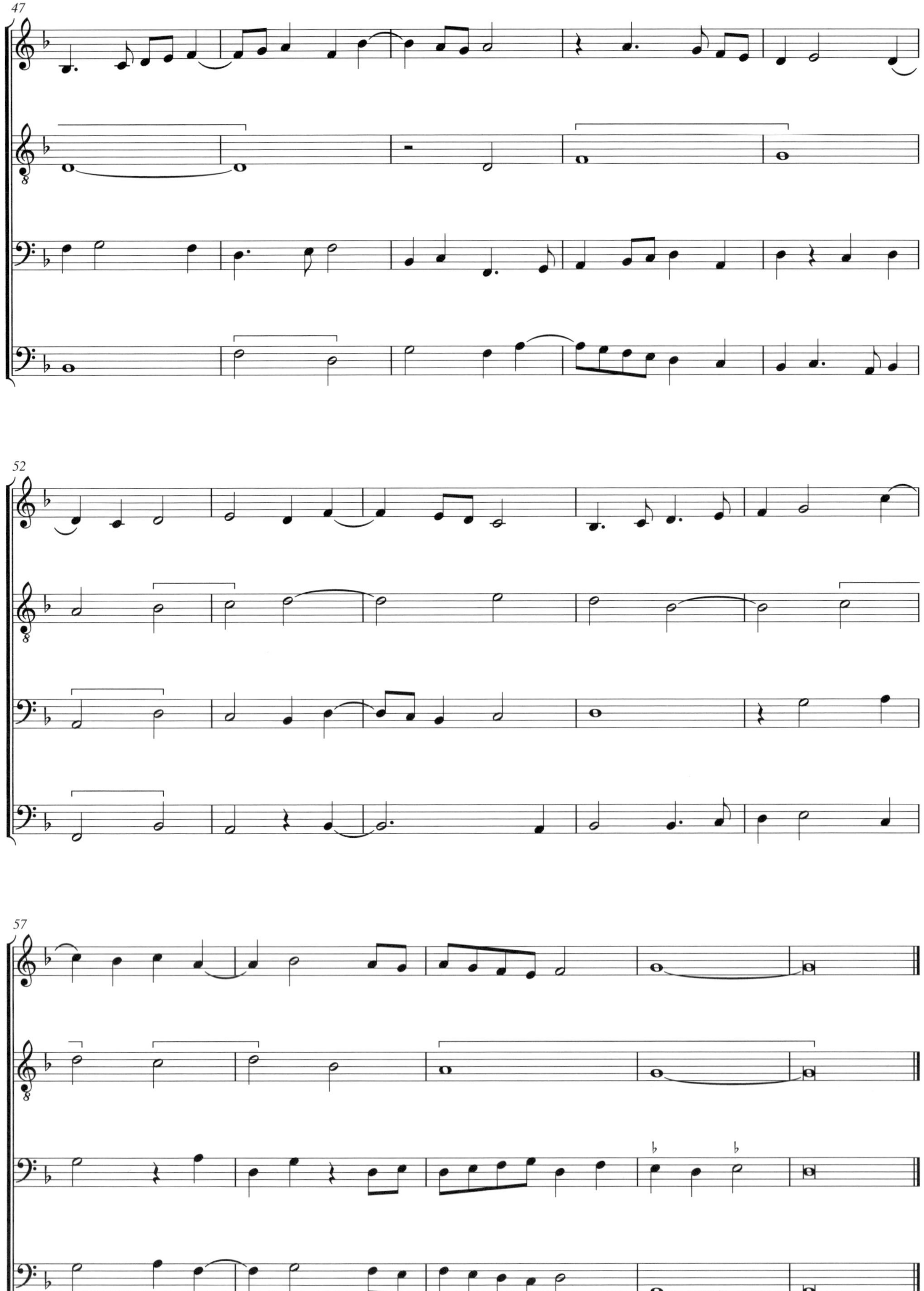
47
52
57

17b. [De tous biens plaine]

Verona 757, fols. 42v–43r

[Alexander Agricola?]

neur. Car as- sou- vy- -e'est en va-

41
-leur Au- tant que ja-
46
- mais, [au- tant
51
que ja- mais] fut de- es-
56
- - - - se.

18. De tous biens

Bologna Q16, fols. 137(a)v–138(a)r

Anonymous

[Superius]

[Tenor]

[D]E tous biens.

DE tous bin plein

[Bassus]

DE tous biens

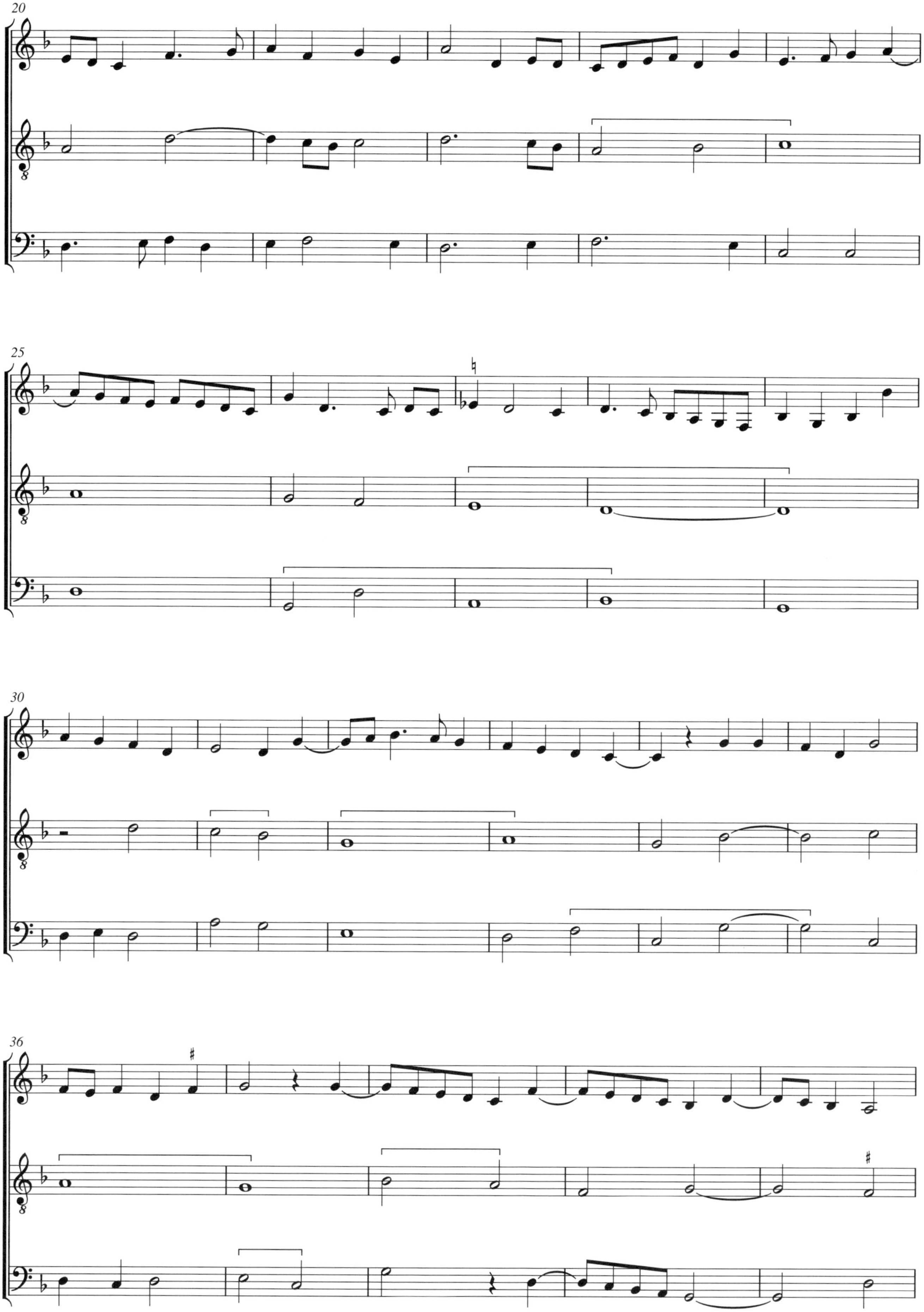
20
25
30
36

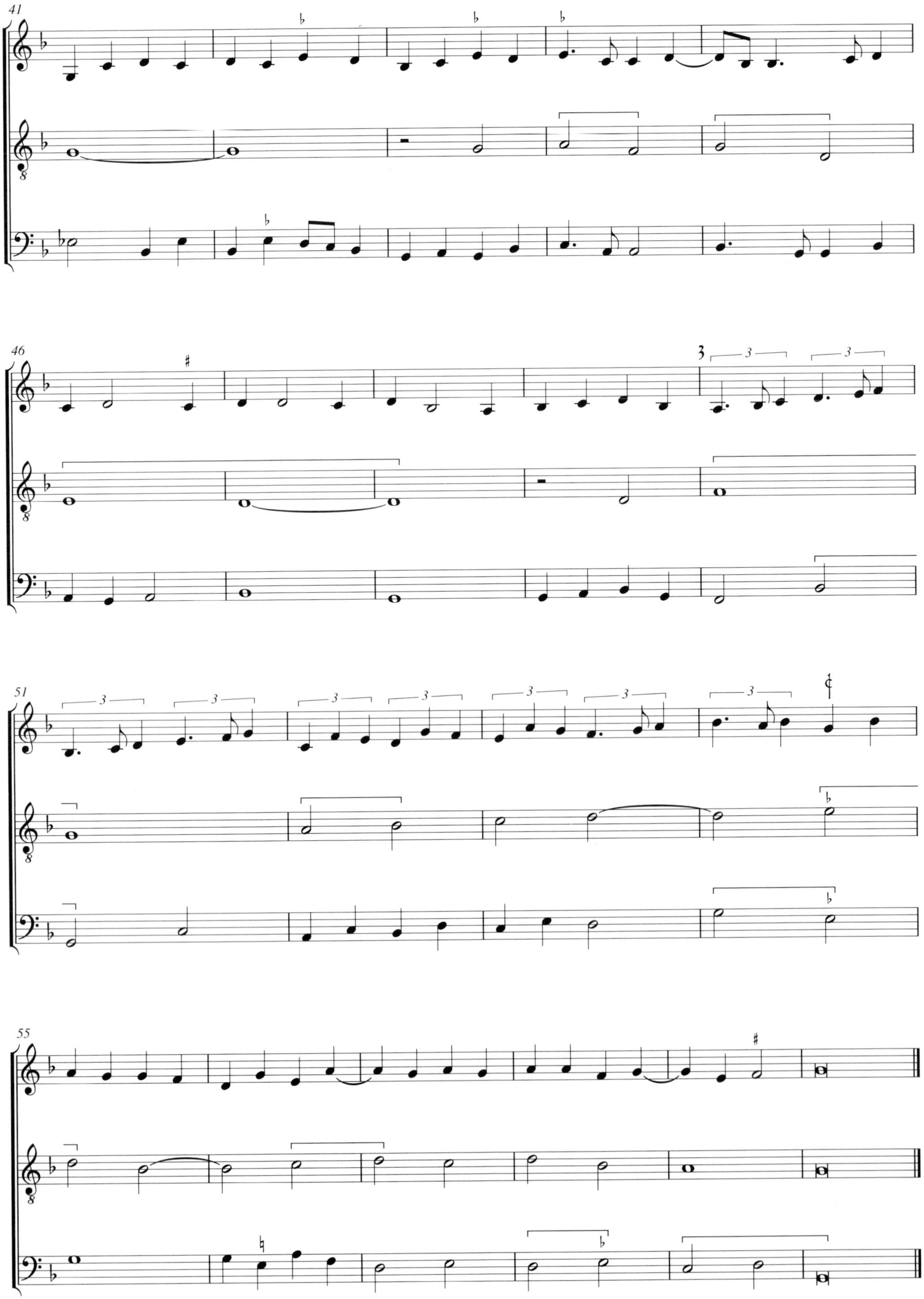

19. De tous biens

Odhecaton, no. 73, fols. 79v–80r

Bourdon/[Alexander Agricola]

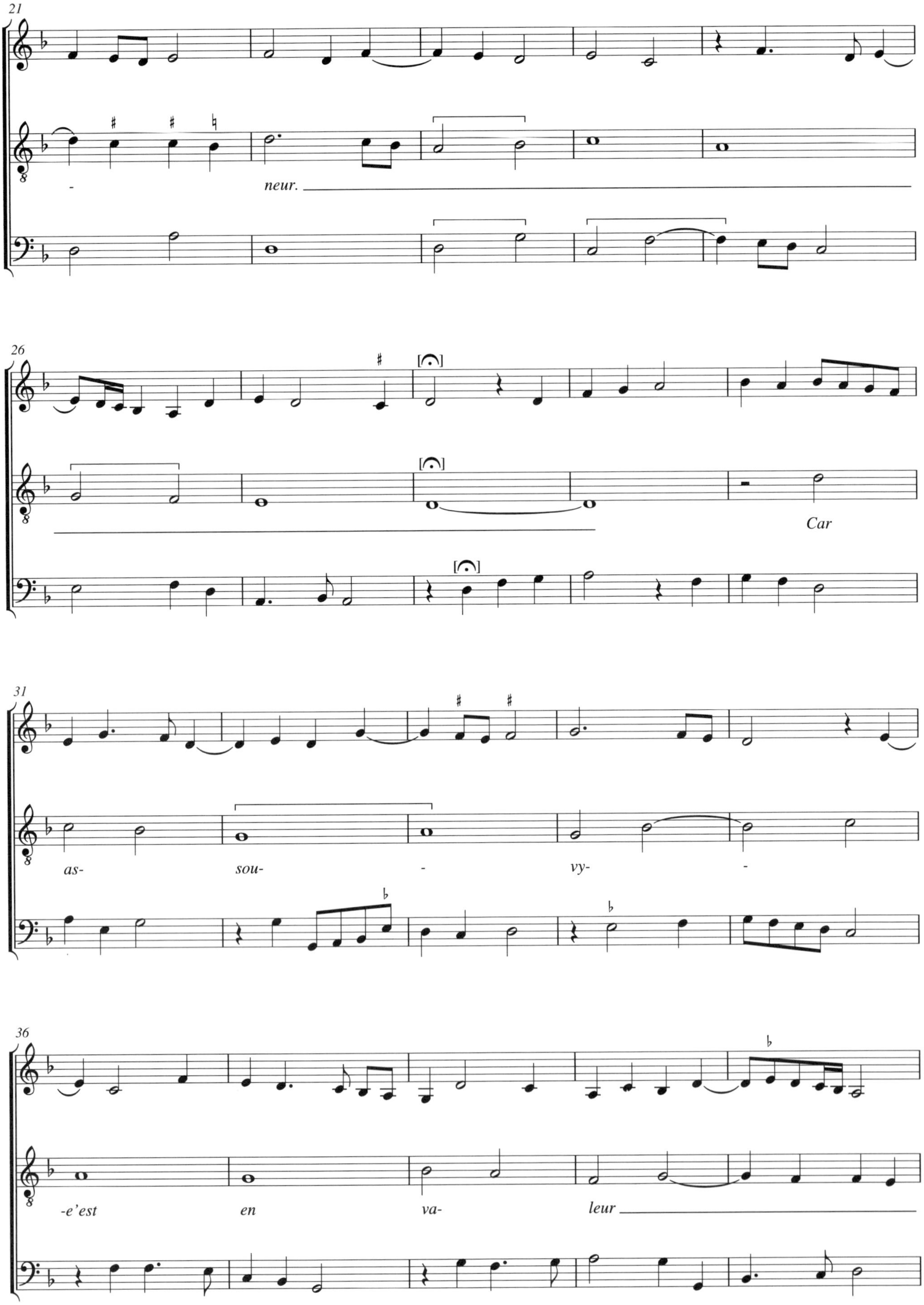
21
neur.
26
Car
31
as-
sou-
vy-
36
-e'est
en
va-
leur

69

20. De tous biens playne

Segovia, fols. 180v–181r

Alexander Agricola

[Superius]

[Tenor]

[D]e tous biens playne

De tous biens playne

[Bassus]

[D]E tous biens playne

71

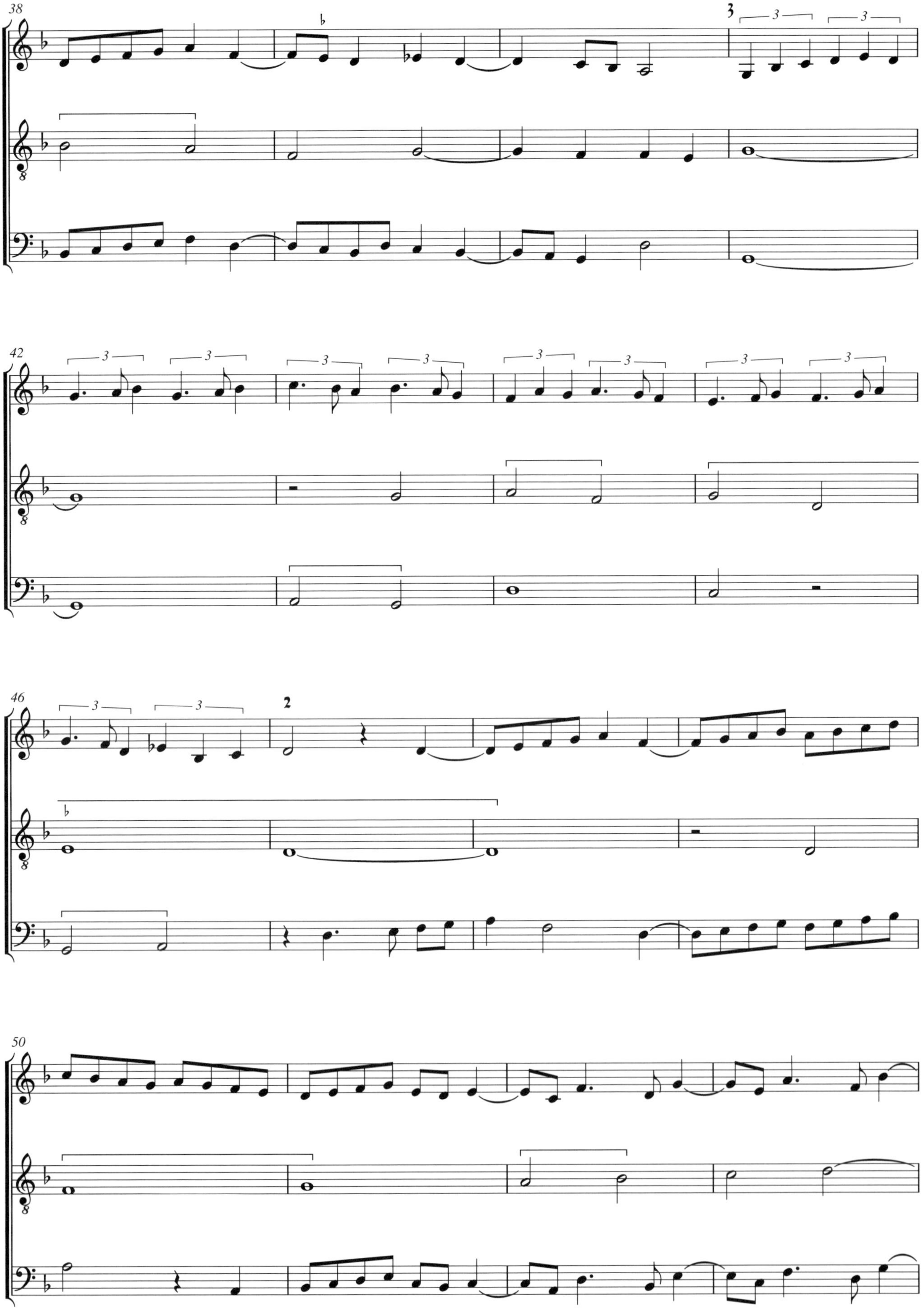
38
3
42
46
2
50

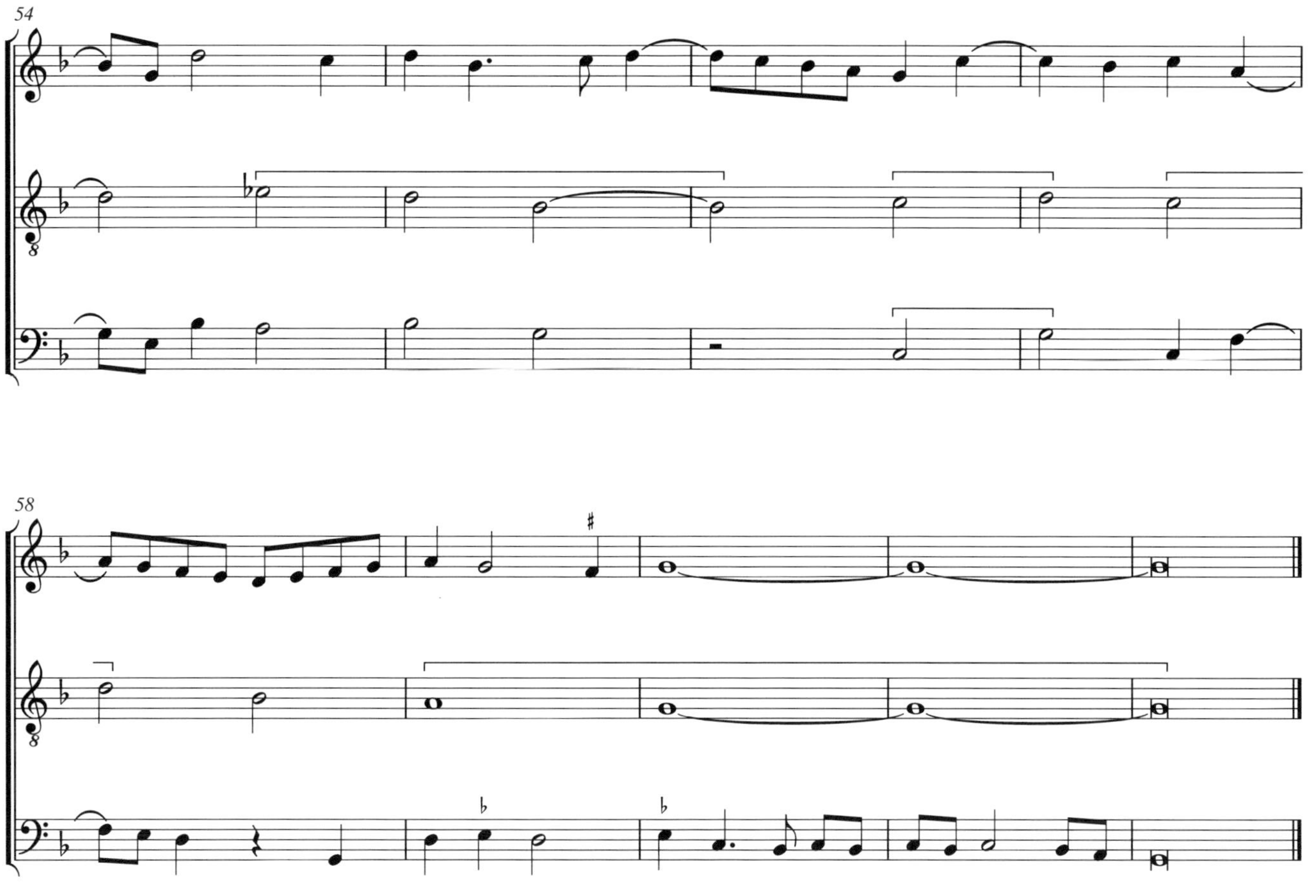
54
58

21. De tous biens playne

Segovia, fols. 194v–195r

Alexander Agricola

[Superius]

[Tenor] De tous biens playne

[Bassus] [D]e tous biens playne

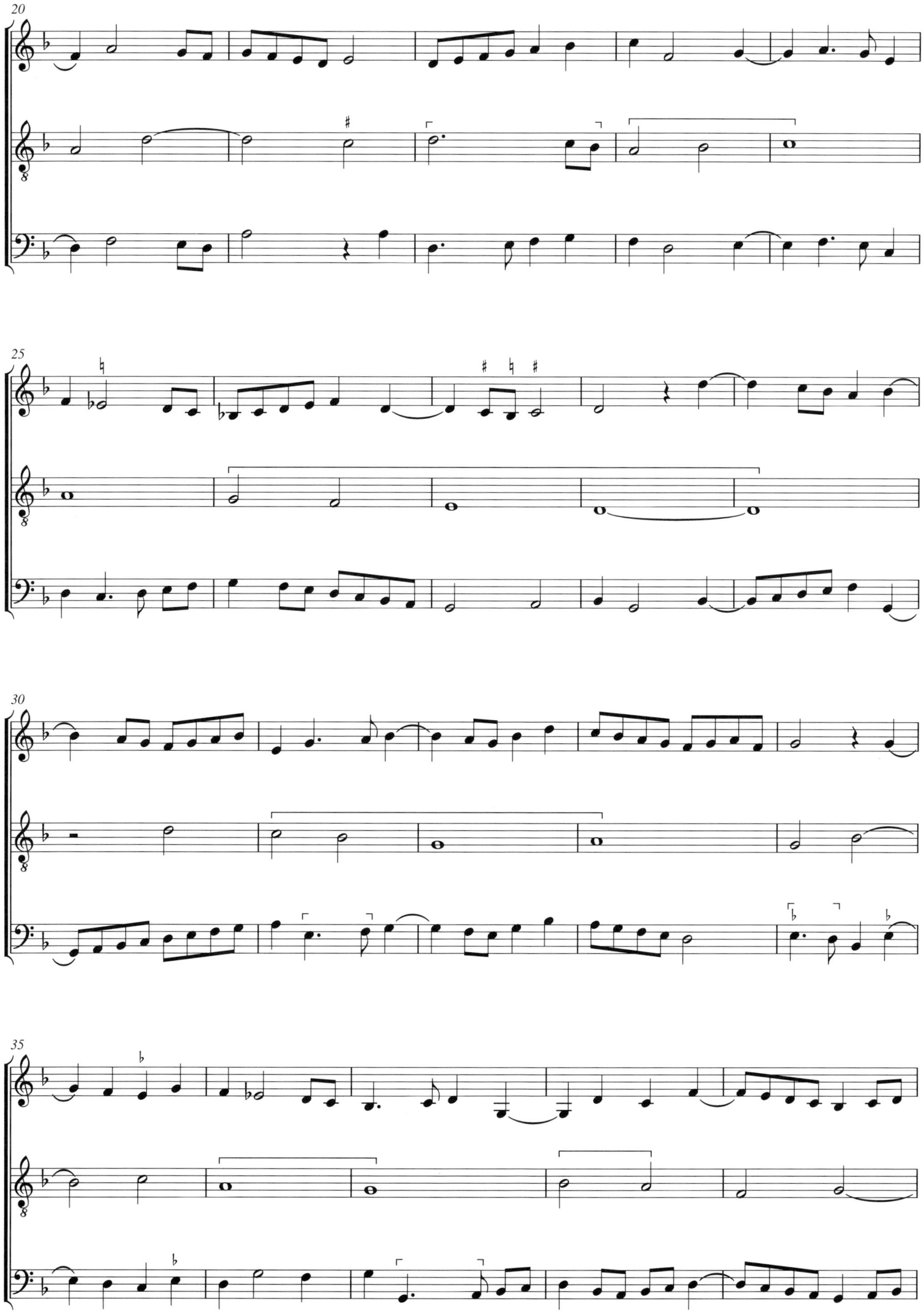
20
25
30
35

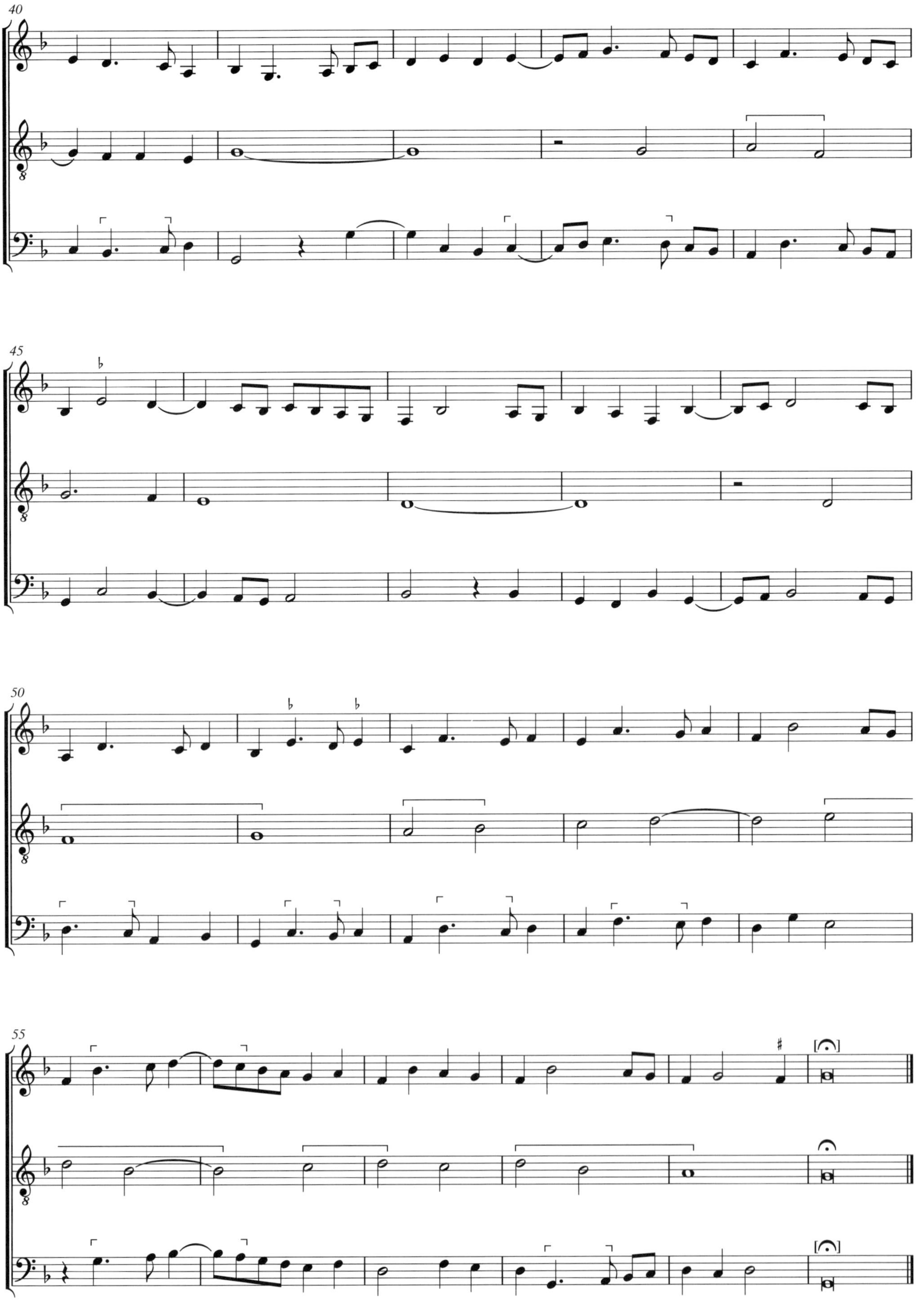
40
45
50
55

22. De tous biens playne

Flor C 2439, fols. 67v–68r

Allexander [Agricola]

[Superius]

Tenor

DE tous biens playne

De tous [biens] playne

Bassus

De tous biens plaine

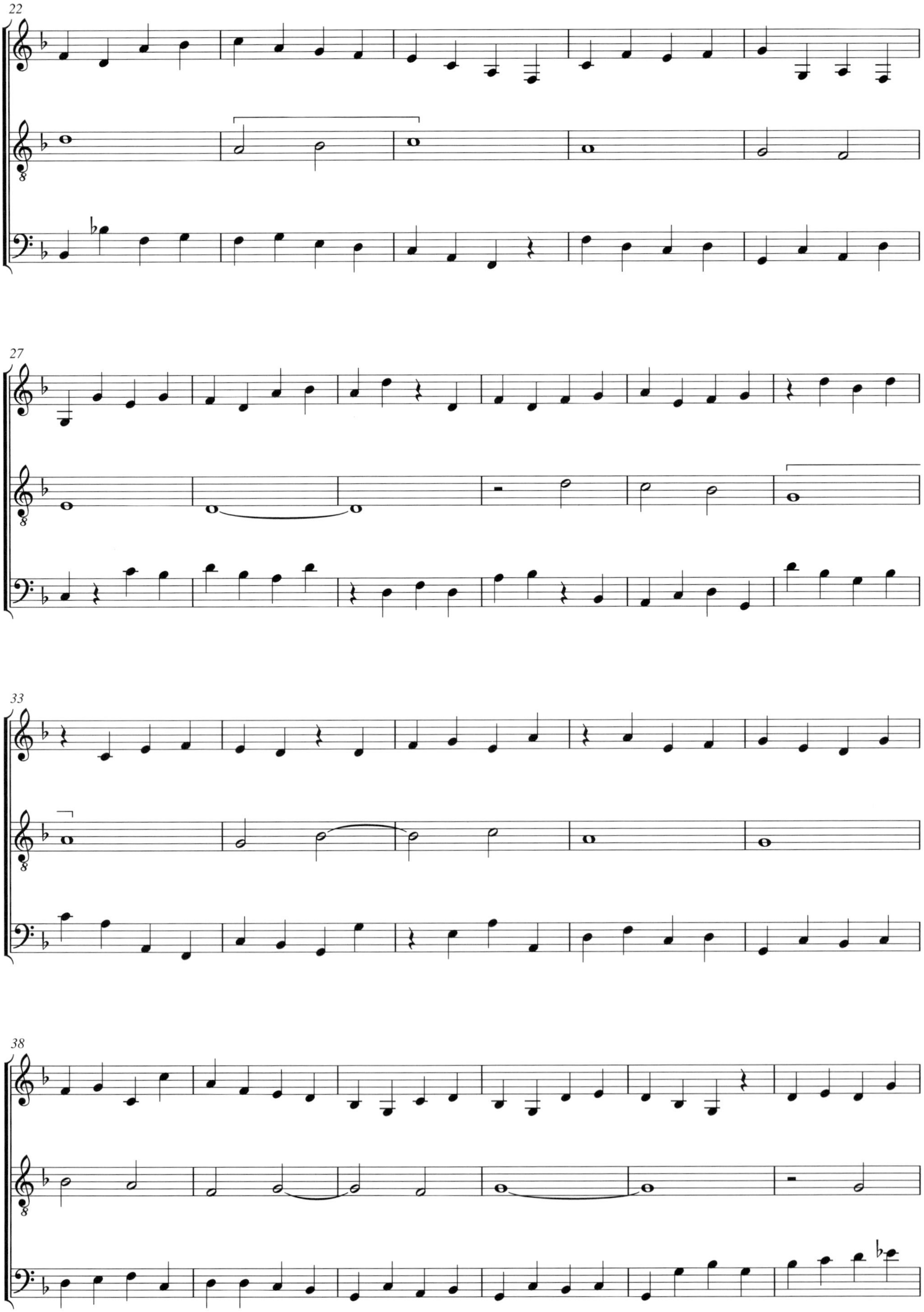

22
27
33
38

79

23. De tous biens playne

Flor C 2439, fols. 66v–67r

Allexander [Agricola]

DE tous biens playne

De tous biens plaine

De tous biens playne

81

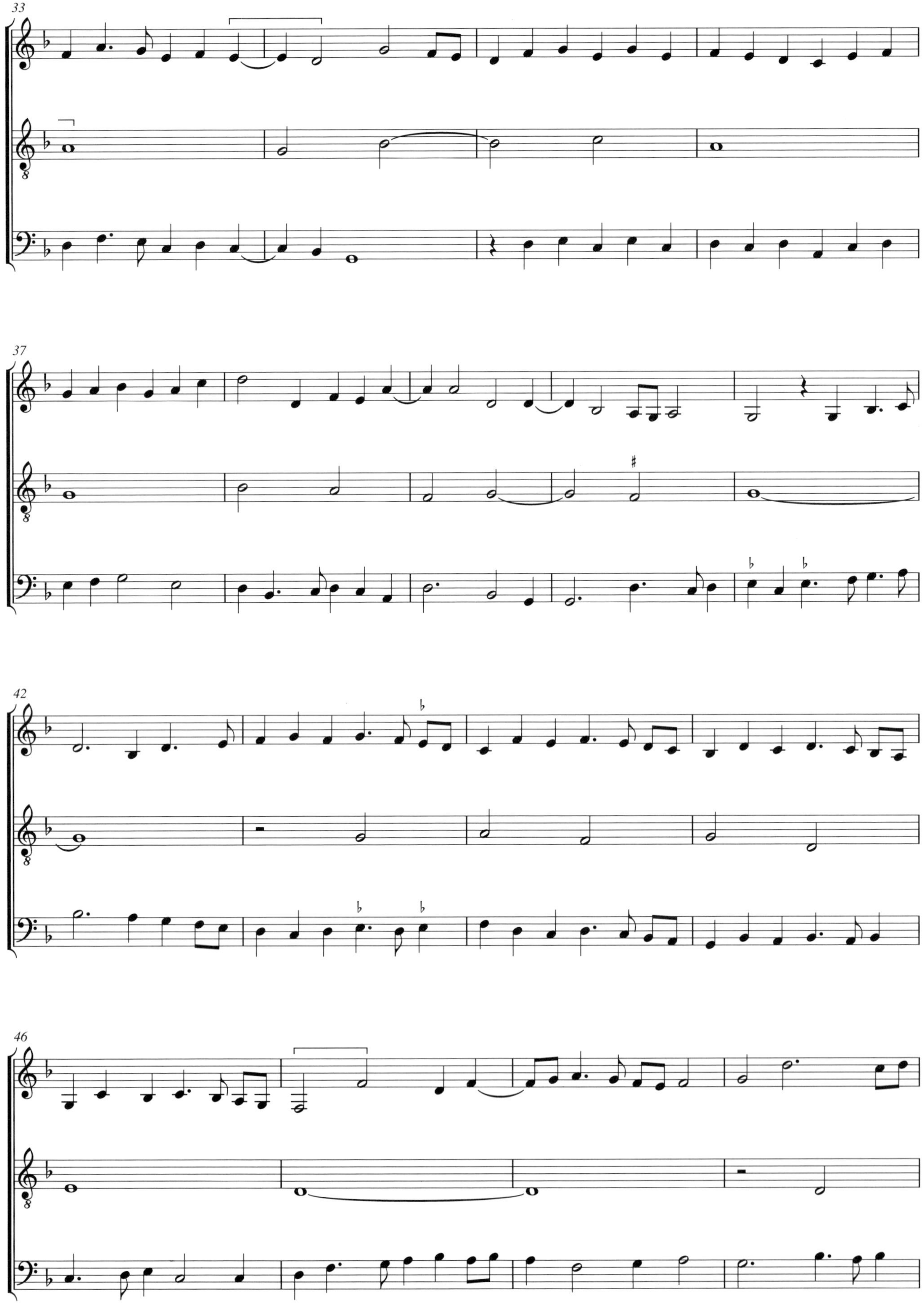
33
37
42
46

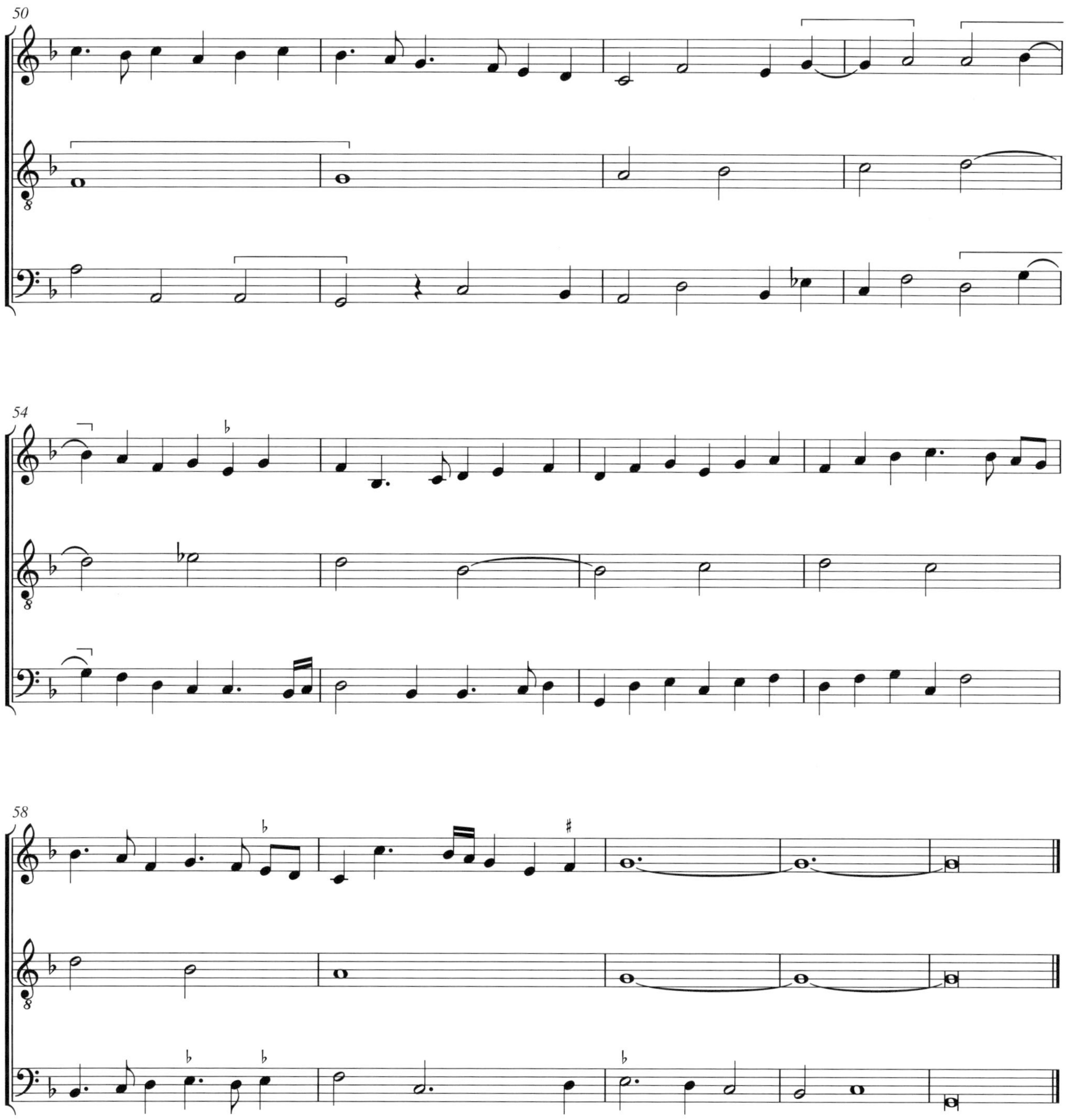
50
54
58

24. De tous biens

Bologna Q17, fols. 26v–27r

Bactio [Bartolomeo degli Organi]

85

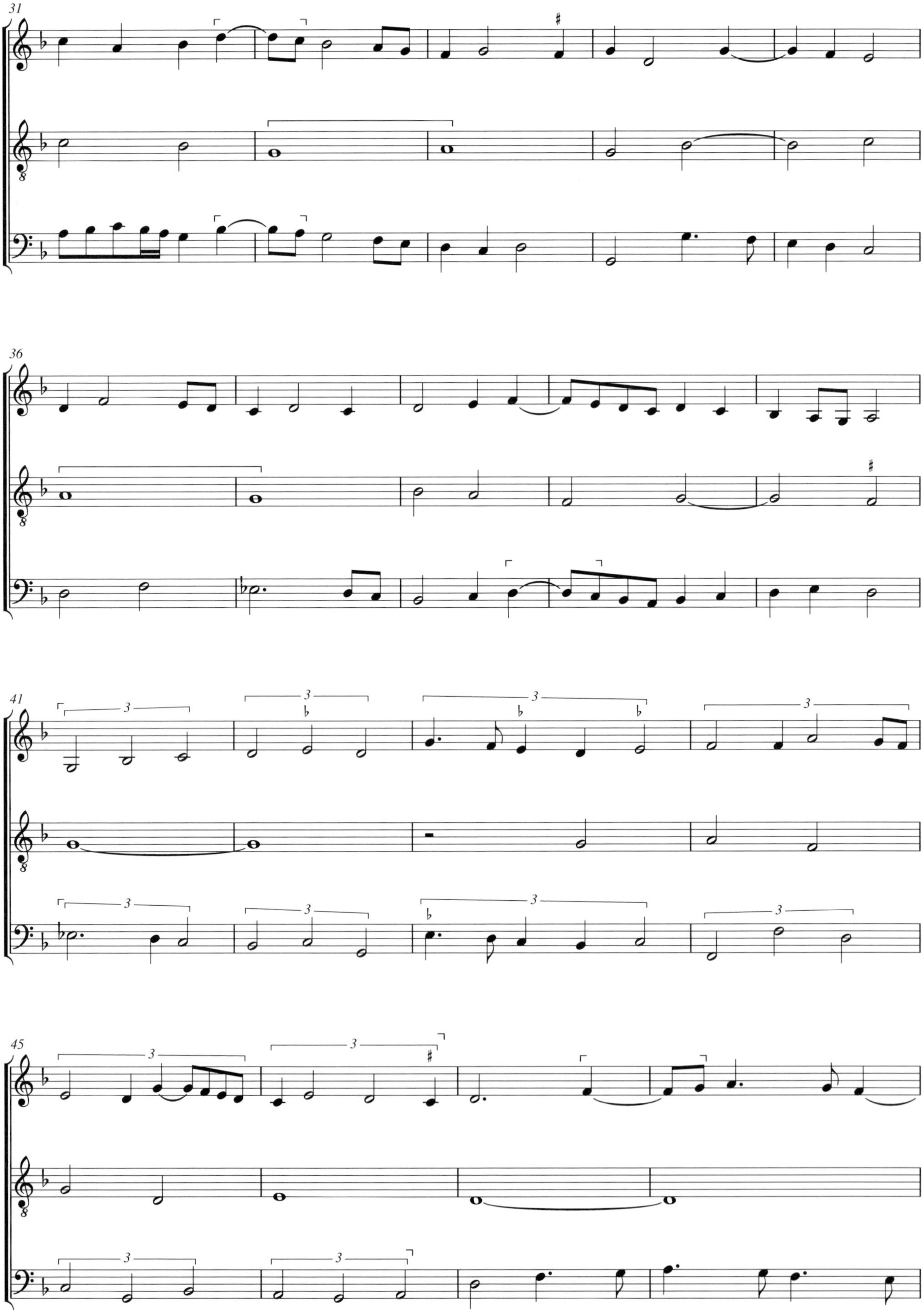

87

25. De to biens playne

CG, fols. 15v–17r (22v–24r)

Anonymous

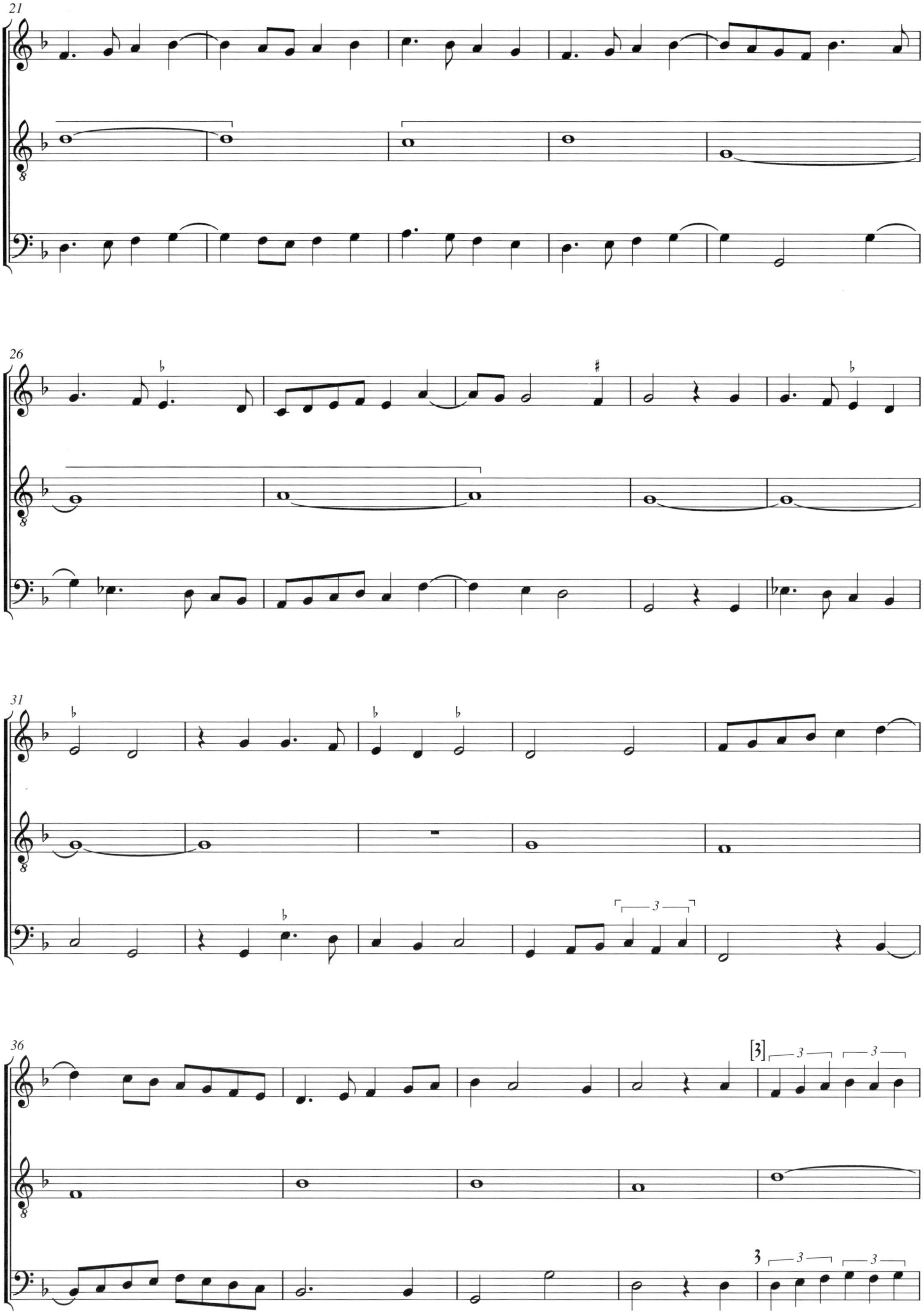
21
26
31
36
[3]
3

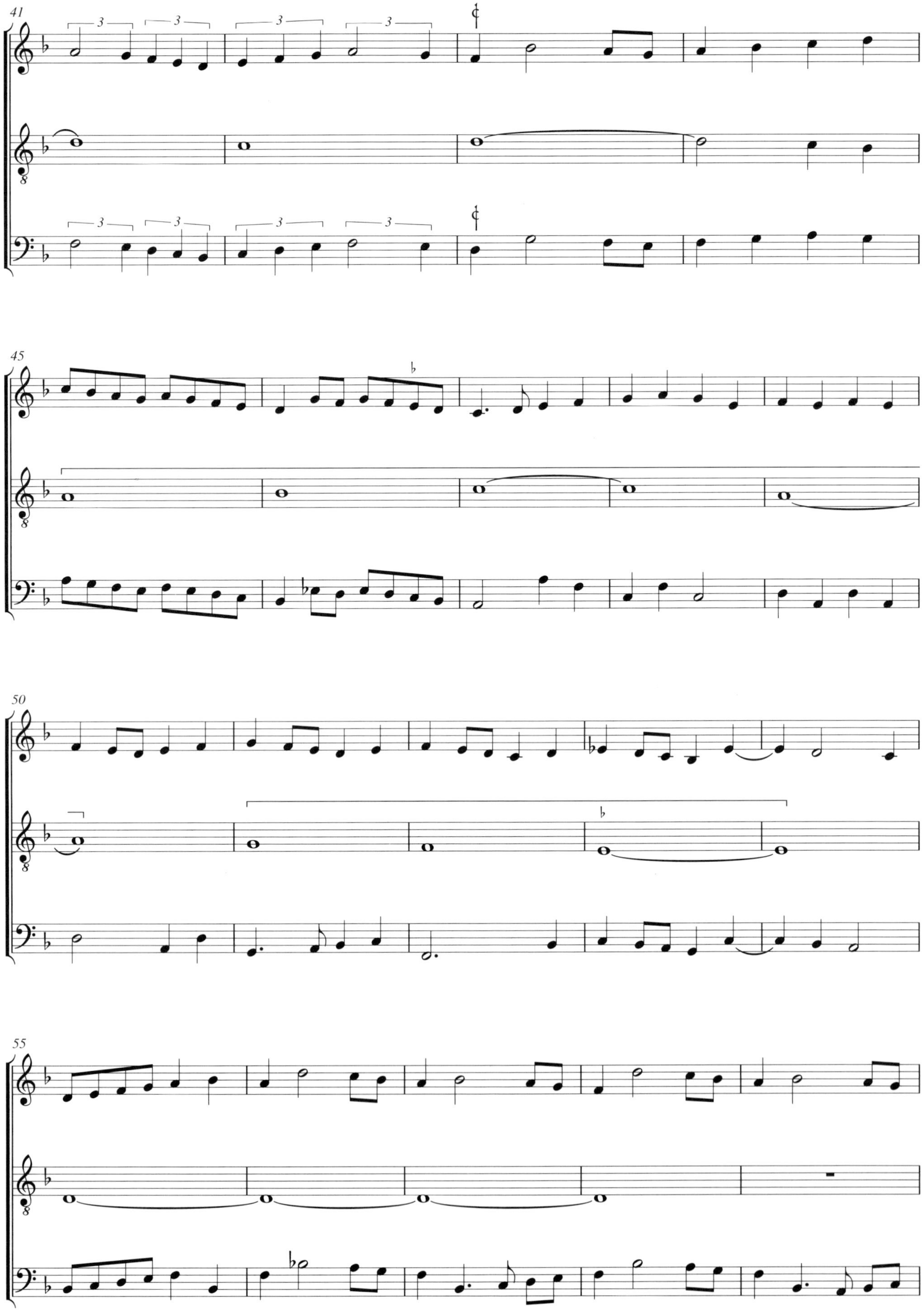
41
3
3
3
3
3
3
3
3
45
50
55

91

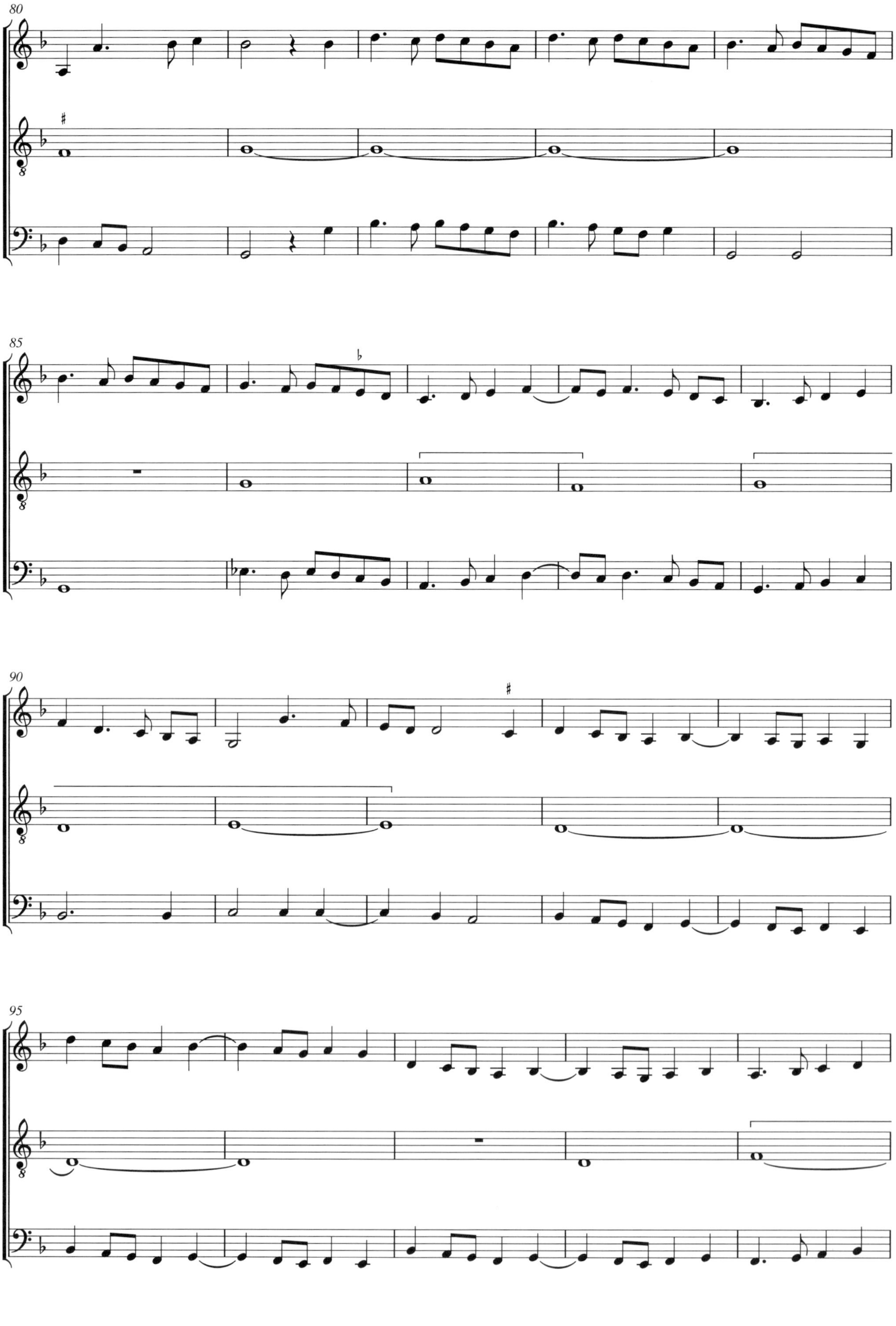
80
85
90
95

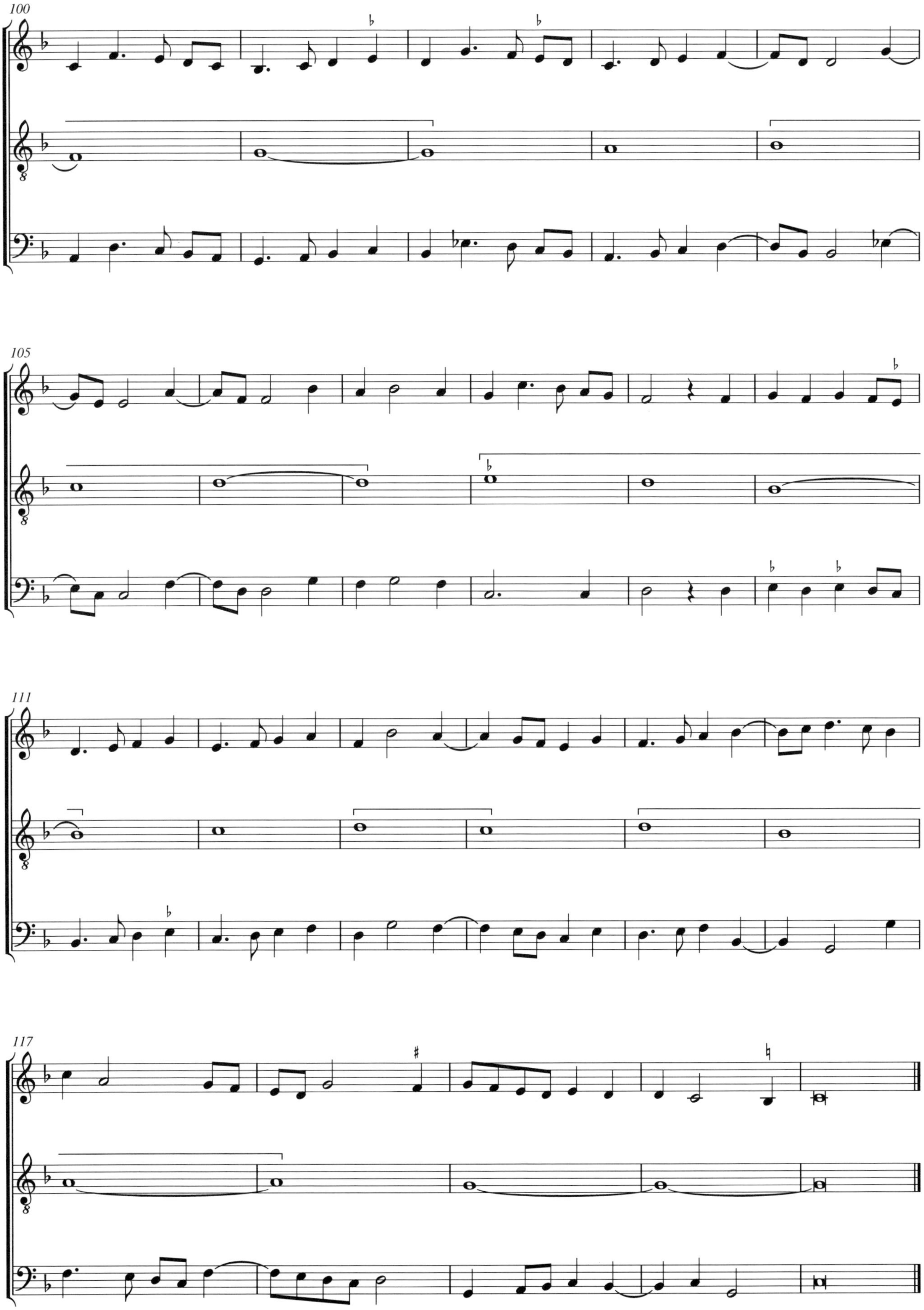
100
105
111
117

26. De tous bien plen

Bologna Q18, fols. 51v–52r

Anonymous

Cha- cun lui doit tri- but d'on- neur.

Car _____ as- sou- vy- -e est en va- -leur _____ Au-

97

se.

27. De tous biens

Canti C, no. 59, fols. 79v–80r

Jo[hannes] Japart

[Superius] DE tous biens

Contra De tous biens

Tenor De tous biens

Bassus De tous biens

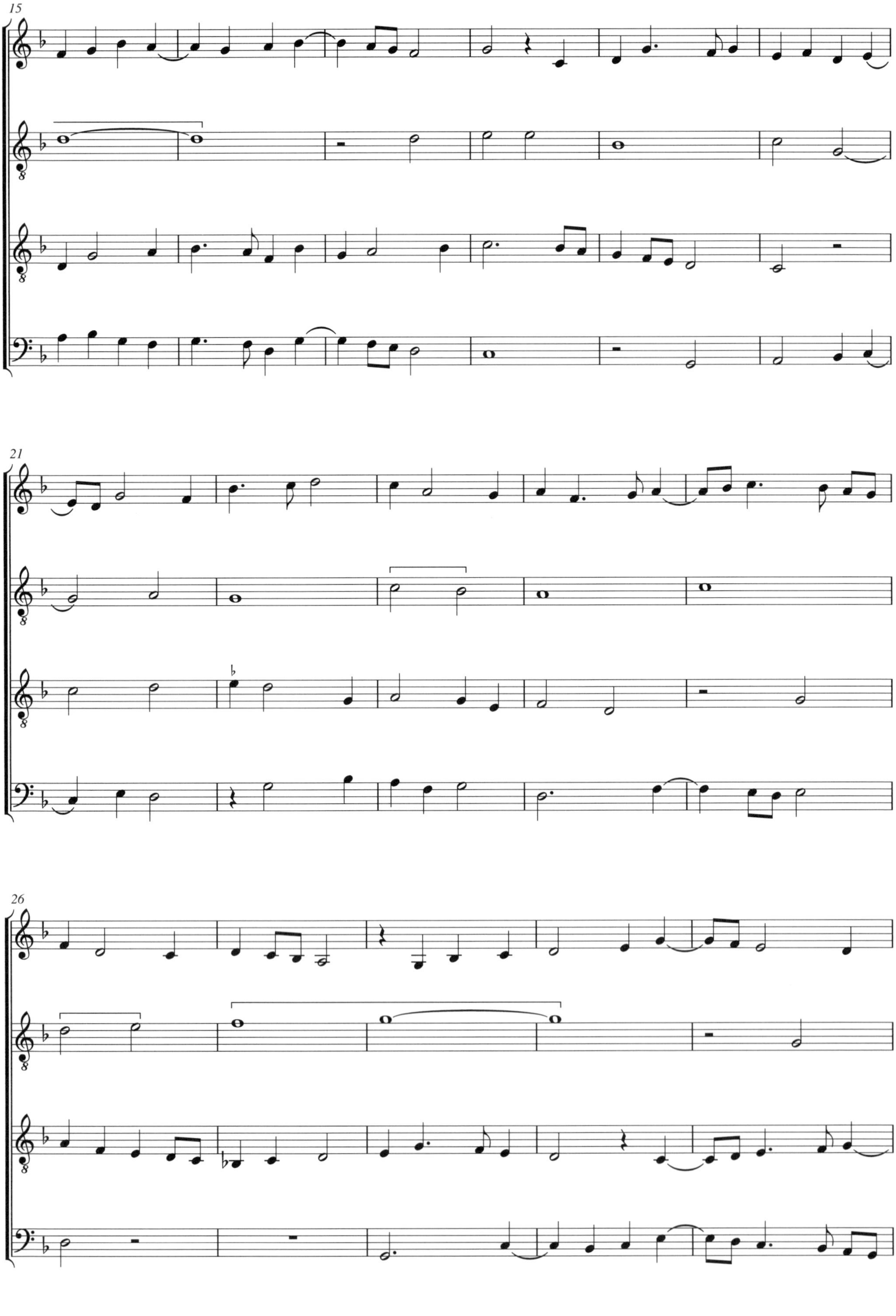
15
21
26

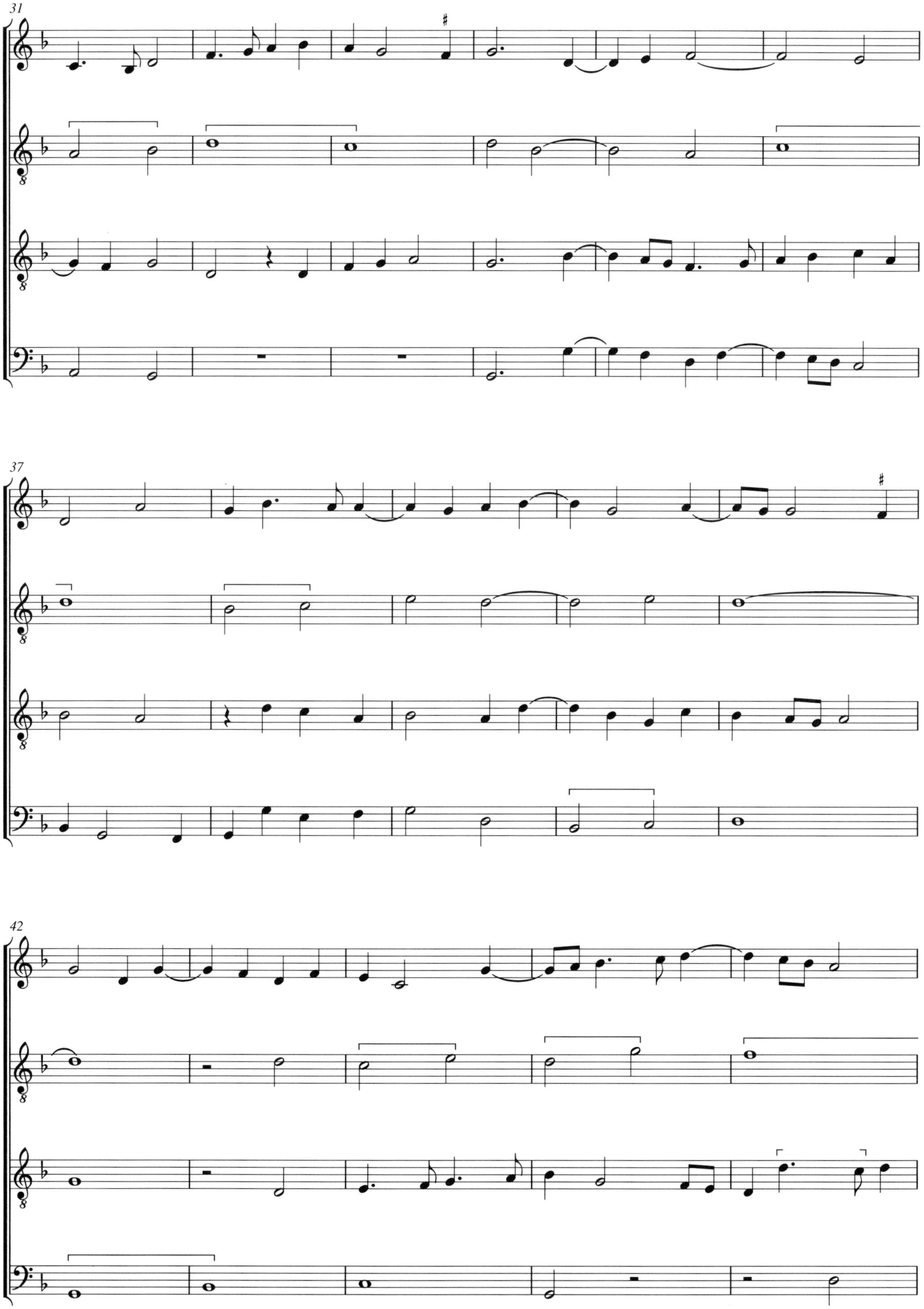
31
37
42

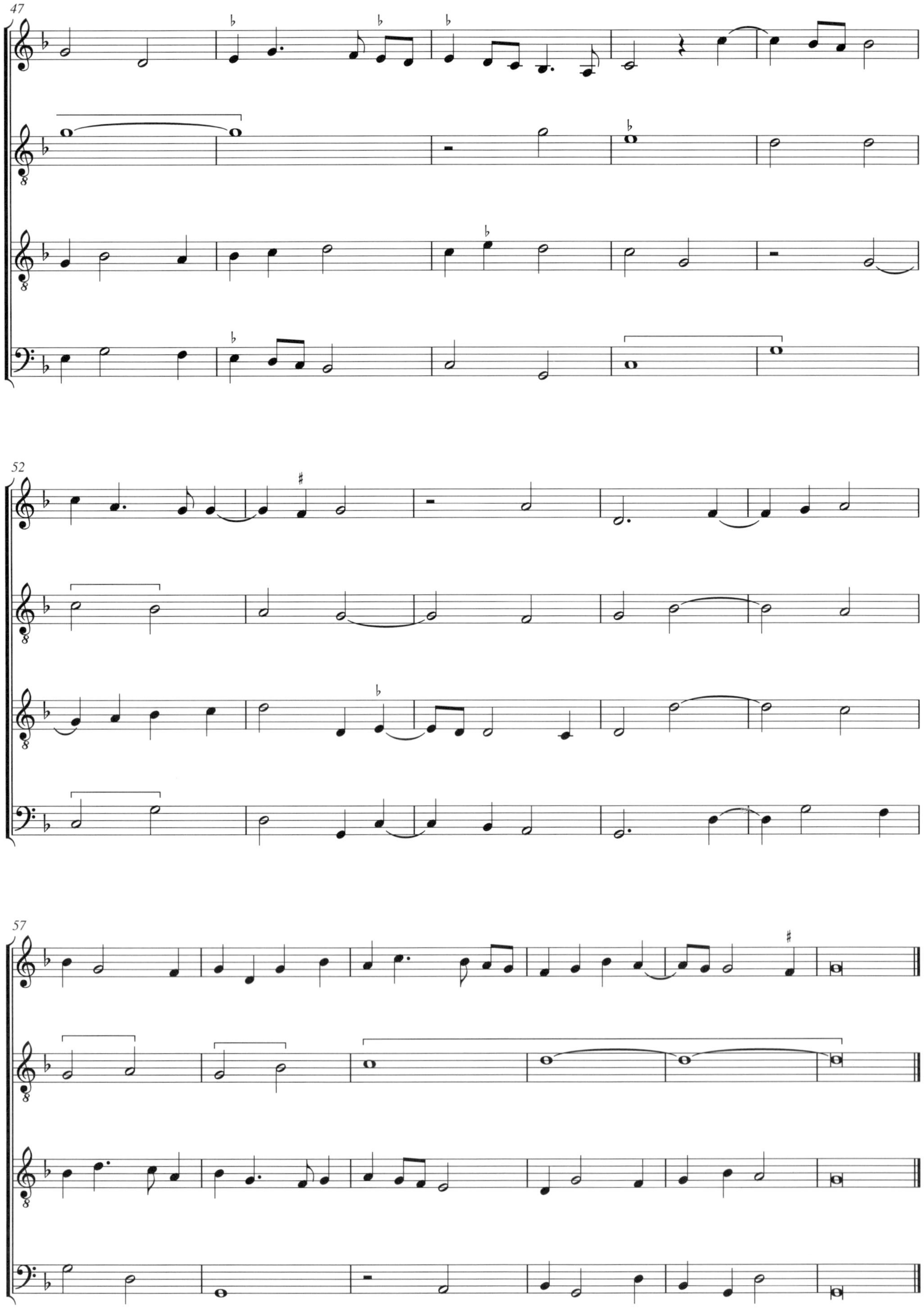
47
52
57

28. De tous biens plaine

Cambrai 125–28, no. 27, fol. 46v

D'Oude Schuere

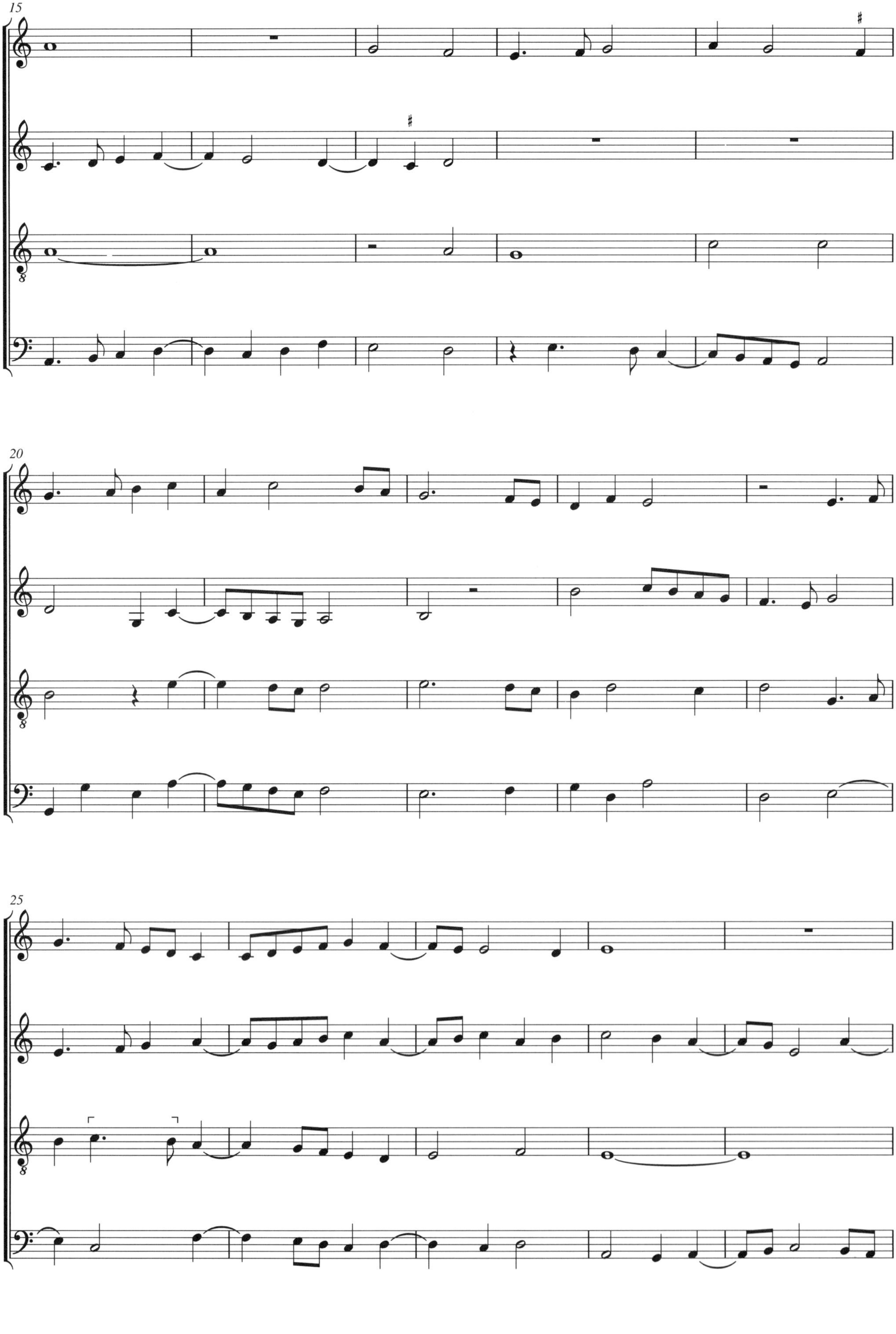
15
20
25

105

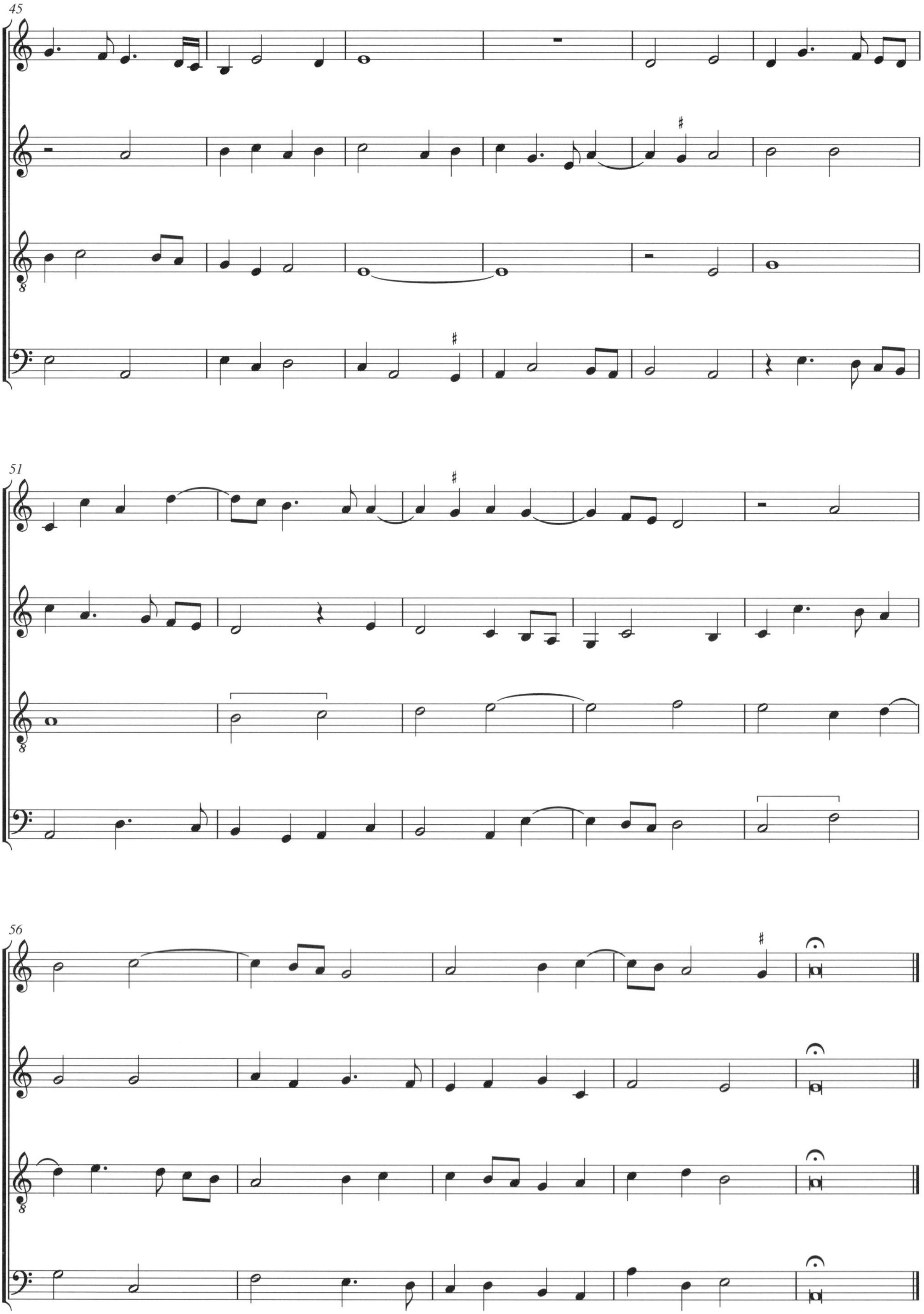
45
51
56

Critical Report

List of Sources

Note: Manuscript sigla and dating are based upon information included in Charles Hamm and Herbert Kellman, eds., *The Census-Catalogue of Manuscript Sources of Polyphonic Music, 1400–1550*, 5 vols., Renaissance Manuscript Studies, no. 1 (Neuhausen-Stuttgart: Hänssler Verlag, 1979–88) unless otherwise noted. Print sources include reference numbers for François Lesure, ed., *Recueils imprimés XVIe–XVIIe siècles*, series B/1 of *Répertoire international des sources musicales* [RISM] (München-Duisburg: G. Henle, 1960).

Augsburg
: Augsburg, Staats- und Stadtbibliothek, MS Mus. 25.
ca. 1500
Setting: fragmentary reworking, probably based on an ornamented paraphrase of the superius.

Banco Rari 229
: Florence, Biblioteca Nazionale Centrale, Banco Rari 229 (*olim* Magliabechi XIX. 59).
1492–93
Settings: 5, 7

Bologna Q16
: Bologna, Civico Museo Bibliografico Musicale, MS Q16 (*olim* 109).
Main corpus finished in 1487, later additions made ca. 1490–1510.
Settings: 1, 18

Bologna Q17
: Bologna, Civico Museo Bibliografico Musicale, MS Q17 (*olim* 148).
1490s; before 1500
Setting: 24

Bologna Q18
: Bologna, Civico Museo Bibliografico Musicale, MS Q18 (*olim* 143).
early 16th century
Settings: 3, 26

Cambrai 125–28
: Cambrai, Bibliothèque municipale, MS 125–128 (*olim* 124) [4 partbooks].
1542
Setting: 28

Canti B
: *Canti B. numero cinquanta B.* Venice: O. Petrucci, 1501.
RISM 1502[2]; 2d ed., 1503[3].
Setting: 11

Canti C
: *Canti C. Numero cento cinquanta.* Venice: O. Petrucci, 1503.
RISM 1504[3].
Settings: 6, 12, 14, 16, 17a, 27

Cape Town
: Cape Town, South African Public Library, MS Grey 3.b.12.
before 1506
Setting: 1

Capirola
: Chicago, Newberry Library, Case MS, VM 140.C25. (*Compositione di meser Vicenzo Capirola, gentil homo bresano*; "Vincenzo Capirola's Lute Book")
ca. 1517[1]
Setting: 11 (non-concordant)

Casanatense
: Rome, Biblioteca Casanatense, MS 2856 (*olim* O.V. 208).
ca. 1485–90
Setting: 1

CG
: Vatican City, Biblioteca Apostolica Vaticana, Cappella Giulia, MS XIII 27. ("Codex Medici")
1492–94
Settings: 1, 9, 16, 17b, 25

Cop 291/8
: Copenhagen, Det Kongelige Bibliotek, MS Thott 291, 8°.
1470–80
Setting: 1

Cop 1848
: Copenhagen, Det Kongelige Bibliotek, MS Ny kongelige Samling, MS 1848, 2°.
ca. 1525
Setting: 1 (non-concordant)

Cordiforme
: Paris, Bibliothèque Nationale, Département de Manuscrits, Collection Rothschild, MS 2973 (shelfmark:

	1.5.13). ("Cordiforme Chansonnier") 1470–77 Setting: 1	Laborde	Washington, Library of Congress, Music Division, MS M.2.1.L25 Case. ("Laborde Chansonnier") ca. 1463–71 Setting: 1
Dijon	Dijon, Bibliothèque municipale, MS 517 (*olim* 295). 1470–75 Setting: 1	Linz	Linz, Bundesstaatliche Studienbibliothek, MS 529. 1485–1500[4] Setting: fragmentary superius-based reworking
Egenolff	Paris, Bibliothèque Nationale, Rés. Vm[7] 504 [Lieder zu 3 und 4 Stimmen. Frankfurt am Main: C. Egenolff, n.d.]. RISM [c. 1535][14]. [3 vols.; only discantus partbook survives.] Settings: 1, 11 (non-concordant)	London 31922	London, British Library, Reference Division, Department of Manuscripts, MS Additional 31922. ("Henry VIII Manuscript") ca. 1510–20 Setting: 1
Flor 121	Florence, Biblioteca Nazionale Centrale, MS Magliabechi XIX. 121. ca. 1500 Setting: 1	Maastricht	Maastricht, Rijksarchief van Limburg, unnumbered musical fragments. ca. 1480 Setting: 1 (superius only)
Flor 178	Florence, Biblioteca Nazionale Centrale, MS Magliabechi XIX. 178. ca. 1492–94 Setting: 1	Mellon	New Haven, Yale University, Beinecke Library for Rare Books and Manuscripts, MS 91. ("Mellon Chansonnier") ca. 1475–76 Setting: 1
Flor C 2439	Florence, Conservatorio di Musica Luigi Cherubini, Biblioteca, MS Basevi 2439. ("Basevi Codex") 1506–14, probably ca. 1508 Settings: 22, 23	Monte Cassino	Monte Cassino, Biblioteca dell'Abbazia, MS 871 (*olim* 871N). ca. 1480–1500 Setting: 1
Flor Panc 27	Florence, Biblioteca Nazionale Centrale, MS Panciatichi 27. early 16th century Setting: 5	*Motetti A*	*Motetti A. numero trentatre.-A*. Venice: O. Petrucci, 1502. RISM 1502[1]. Setting: 10
Formschneider	*Trium vocum carmina a diversis musicis composita*. Nuremberg: H. Formschneider, 1538. RISM 1538[9]. Settings: 1 (non-concordant), 16	Mun 239	Munich, Universitätsbibliothek der Ludwig-Maximilians-Universität, MS 2º Art. 239. 1514–17 Settings: 1 (non-concordant), 8
Fribourg	Fribourg, Bibliothèque Cantonale et Universitaire, MS Cap. Res. 527 (formerly Kapuziner-Kloster, MS Falk Z 105). ca. 1500[2] Setting: 1 (intabulation)	Mun 3154	Munich, Bayerische Staatsbibliothek, Musiksammlung, Musica MS 3154. ("Chorbuch des Nikolaus Leopold") ca. 1466–1511 Setting: 13
Glareanus	Glareanus, Heinrich. *Dodecachordon*. Basel, 1547. RISM 1547[1]. Setting: 8	Newsidler	*Der ander Theil des Lautenbuchs ... Hansen Newsidler Lutinisten*. Nuremberg: J. Petreius, 1536. RISM 1536[13]. Setting: 11 (intabulation)
Kassel	Kassel, Murhard'sche Bibliothek der Stadt Kassel und Landesbibliothek, MS 8º Mus. 53/2 [only discantus partbook survives].[3] mid-16th century Setting: 1 (superius only)	*Odhecaton*	*Harmonice musices Odhecaton A*. Venice: O. Petrucci, 1501. RISM 1501, 1503[2], 1504[2]. Settings: 2, 8, 19

Paris 676	Paris, Bibliothèque Nationale, Département de Musique, Fonds du Conservatoire, MS Rés. Vm[7] 676. 1502 Setting: 1
Pavia 362	Pavia, Biblioteca Universitaria, MS Aldini 362 (*olim* 131.A.17). Late 1460s or early 1470s; additions made by a later hand. Setting: 1
Perugia 431	Perugia, Biblioteca Comunale Augusta, MS 431 (G.20). 1480–90, probably ca. 1485 Setting: 1
Perugia 1013	Perugia, Biblioteca Comunale Augusta, MS 1013 (M.36). 1509 Settings: 20 (non-concordant), 23
Pesaro	Pesaro, Biblioteca Comunale Oliveriana, MS 1144 (*olim* 1193). ca. 1500[5] Setting: 1 (intabulation)
Pixérécourt	Paris, Bibliothèque Nationale, Département des Manuscrits, Fonds Français, MS 15123 (*olim* Suppl. Fr. 2637). ("Pixérécourt Chansonnier") probably ca. 1480–84 Setting: 1
Ricc 2356	Florence, Biblioteca Riccardiana, MS 2356. ca. 1480–85, or late 15th century, with additions in 1540s Setting: 1
Ricc 2794	Florence, Biblioteca Riccardiana, MS 2794. 1480s, probably before 1488 Setting: 1
Schöffer	[Songbook]. Mainz: P. Schöffer, 1513. RISM 1513[2]. Setting: 11 (non-concordant)
Segovia	Segovia, Archivo Capitular de la Catedral, MS s.s. 1500–1503, probably 1502 Settings: 19, 20, 21
Sev/P	Seville, Catedral Metropolitana, Biblioteca Capitular y Colombina, MS 5-1-43 (*olim* Z Tab.135, N.º 33) and Paris, Bibliothèque Nationale, Département des Manuscrits, Nouvelles Acquisitions Français, MS 4379. ca. 1470–85 Setting: 1
Spinacino 1	*Intabolatura de lauto libro primo [Francesco Spinacino]*. Venice: O. Petrucci, 1507. RISM 1507[5]. Setting: 1 (intabulation)
Spinacino 2	*Intabolatura de lauto. Libro secondo [Francesco Spinacino]*. Venice: O. Petrucci, 1507. RISM 1507[6]. Setting: 1 (intabulation)
Ulm 237	Ulm, Münster Bibliothek, Von Schemar'sche Familienstiftung, MS 237 (a–d) [4 partbooks]. ca. 1530–40 Setting: 1
Uppsala 76a	Uppsala, Universitetsbiblioteket, MS Vokalmusik i Handskrift 76a. ca. 1490–1520 Setting: 1
Verona 757	Verona, Biblioteca Capitolare, MS DCCLVII. ca. 1500 Settings: 15, 17b, fragmentary tenor-based reworking
Wolfenbüttel	Wolfenbüttel, Herzog August Bibliothek, MS Guelferbytanus 287 Extravagantium. ca. 1461–65 Setting: 1

List of Works Cited

Modern Editions

AgricOO	Agricola, Alexandri. *Opera Omnia*. Edited by Edward Lerner. Vol. 5, *Cantiones, Musica Instrumentalis, Opera Dubia*. Corpus mensurabilis musicae, vol. 22. N.p.: American Institute of Musicology, 1970.
GhiselinOO	Ghiselin-Verbonnet, Johannes. *Opera Omnia*. Edited by Clytus Gottwald. Vol. 4. Corpus mensurabilis musicae, vol. 23. N.p.: American Institute of Musicology, 1968.
HayneOO	Hayne van Ghizeghem. *Opera Omnia*. Edited by Barton Hudson. Corpus Mensurabilis Musicae, vol. 74. N.p.: American Institute of Musicology, 1977.
Hewitt	*Harmonice musices Odhecaton A*. Edited by Helen Hewitt. Literary texts edited by Isabel Pope. Mediaeval Academy of America Publication 42, Studies and Documents, no. 5. Cambridge,

MA: Mediaeval Academy of America, 1942. Reprint, New York: Da Capo Press, 1978. (Concordance list found on pp. 137–39.)

Secondary Literature

Brown   Brown, Howard Mayer. *Music in the French Secular Theater, 1400–1550.* Cambridge, MA: Harvard University Press, 1963. (Concordance list found on pp. 204–6.)

Fallows   Fallows, David. *A Catalogue of Polyphonic Songs, 1415–1480.* Oxford and New York: Oxford University Press, 1999. (Concordance list found on pp. 129–30.)

Meconi   Meconi, Honey. "Art-Song Reworkings: An Overview." *Journal of the Royal Musical Association* 119 (1994): 1–42.

Editorial Methods

A single source, chosen according to accuracy and rough chronological priority, serves as the basis for each transcription. When faced with comparable sources, the editor has avoided scholarly redundancy by choosing a previously unedited version as the primary source. The critical commentary lists significant differences between concordant sources, particularly in the area of accidentals. Minimal variations among concordant readings involving cadential ornaments, the addition or subtraction of a tie in transcription, or the replacement of a larger note value by two or more smaller ones at the same pitch (and vice versa) have generally not been recorded.

The incipit for each piece indicates the original clef, key signature, and mensuration sign (if provided) and provides the first pitch or neume from the original notation. The incipit also provides the voice designation; when given in brackets, the designation has been supplied by the editor following labels in concordant sources, conventions of voice placement in choirbook format, or association of clef and voice part. The melodic ambitus for each voice part is given in small noteheads following the modern clef, key signature, and time signature.

Without regard to the designation of a voice part, (a) parts originally in any G clef or C1 or C2 (C on the first or second line respectively) are transcribed in treble clef; (b) parts originally in C3 or C4 clefs are transcribed in transposed treble clef; and (c) parts originally in C5 or F clefs are transcribed in bass clef.

The verbal incipit or refrain text for each part as found in the principal source appears in regular typeface underneath the modern transcription. Original spellings have normally been retained, but the modernizations of *i* to *j* and *v* to *u* as well as the expansion of abbreviations and the addition of modern-day punctuation have been made without comment. Elisions are indicated with an apostrophe. Text has been supplied in those reworkings which retain an obvious medial cadence and so lend themselves to a sung performance. Italic type indicates text supplied by the editor. Lamentably, even fully texted sources give only a vague indication of text placement; the editor has tried to respect melodic profile and, to a lesser extent, ligature placement in determining underlay. Heavily ligated tenor parts have on occasion been supplied with text in violation of the convention of one syllable per neume in order to give performers the option of texted performance.

Note values have been halved throughout the edition, with the breve rendered as a whole note and all other values derived accordingly. Rhythms have frequently been renotated (e.g., as tied notes) without comment to reflect the rhythmic pulse. Similarly, the unmeasured long at the end of the piece has been extended as necessary to conform to modern notational conventions. Bar lines have been added to permit easy reading by singers and instrumentalists, and fermatas have been added to clarify the underlying rondeau structure except in settings where that structure no longer obtains.

Coloration, the blackened notation which indicates triple divisions or dotted figures, has been indicated by open horizontal brackets, while ligatures are represented by closed horizontal brackets. Variations in coloration and ligature placement in the concordant readings presumably reflect scribal habit and so are omitted from the critical commentary.

Accidentals in the source have been adjusted to reflect modern conventions. Accidentals appear adjacent to the note they affect regardless of their original placement in the source (where they may appear three or four notes early as precautionary signs). Sharp signs have been modernized to natural signs where appropriate. Redundant accidentals, however, have been retained. The critical commentary mentions any conflicting accidentals in concordant sources. All editorial accidentals, including cancellations and adjustments to follow concordant readings, have been added above the pitch affected. The editor has been governed by the traditional rules of musica ficta and has endeavored to avoid melodic and harmonic tritones, to provide proper cadential motion with its requisite imperfect-to-perfect gesture, to avoid mi contra fa clashes, and to respect the logical hexachordal solmization of individual melodic lines.

Musical and textual material supplied by the editor appears inside full brackets. Other changes or added pitches and rests are indicated in the critical commentary, as are significant variations in the concordant readings.

Critical Commentary

Attributions supplied by the editor or taken from concordant sources have been enclosed in brackets. For each piece, the commentary indicates the composer, the number of parts, and the voice(s) retained from the model. The numbering of the work in the lists published in Brown, HayneOO, and Meconi is given. The entries for the primary source, concordant sources, intabulations, and non-concordant sources give foliation, any attribution as it appears in the source, the textual incipit, an indication of texting for each part, and information about the index entry as appropriate. Comments and notes are provided in temporal order.

The following abbreviations are used in the commentary: S = superius; C = cantus; A = altus; CT = contra(tenor); T = tenor/middle voice; B = bassus/lowest part; anon = anonymous; m(m). = measure(s); no. = number; fol(s). = folio(s); p(p). = page(s); br = breve; sbr = semibreve; min = minim; smin = semiminim. Pitches are given according to the system in which c' refers to middle C. References to notes, whether tied or not, and rests are counted from the beginning of each measure in the appropriate voice. Thus, a reference to m. 52, T, notes 3–4 would be to measure 52, tenor voice, the third and fourth notes/rests. Texting is indicated with the following abbreviations: t = texted, including *residuum*; r = refrain only; i = incipit only; x = textless.

1. *De tous biens plaine*

[Hayne van Ghizeghem]
a 3; model

Inventory numbers. Brown d; HayneOO 6a; Meconi 1.

SOURCES

Primary source. Laborde, fols. 62v–63r, anon, De tous biens plaine, t–i–i; index: De tous biens plaine.

Concordant sources. Bologna Q16, fols. 133v–134r, anon, De tous biens plen, i–i–i; index: De tus bien plen; Dragan Plamenac erroneously cites fols. 132v–133r; see idem, "The 'Second' Chansonnier of the Biblioteca Riccardiana (Codex 2356)," *Annales musicologiques* 2 (1954): 138–39. Cape Town, fols. 84v–85r, anon, Cum defecerint, substitute text–i–i; the substitute text is Prov. 26:20, 22 (see HayneOO, xxxviii); Brown inadvertently omitted this concordance in his inventory of Uppsala 76a; see idem, "A 'New' Chansonnier of the Early Sixteenth Century in the University Library of Uppsala: A Preliminary Report," *Musica Disciplina* 37 (1983): 200–201. Casanatense, fols. 66v–67r, Haine, De to[us] biens plaine, i–i–i; index: De to[us] biens plaini. CG, fols. 57v–58r (64v–65r), anon, De to biens plena, i–x–x; index: De To biens plaine; shares a superius with a three-voice reworking found on the same opening (see discussion of setting 9); Brown and others incorrectly identify this as part of a setting *a 5*. Cop 291/8, fols. 5v–6r, anon, De tous biens plaine, t–i–x. Cordiforme, fols. 25v–26r, anon, De tous biens plaine, t–i–i; index: De tous biens plaine. Dijon, fols. 14v–15r, Hayne, De tous biens plaine, t–i–i; index: de tous biens plaine; Brown claims the piece is on fol. 11v; see idem, "A 'New' Chansonnier," 200–201. Egenolff, III, no. 16, anon, De tous biens, i– [superius partbook only]. Flor 121, fols. 24v–25r, anon, De tus bem plaine, i–x–x. Flor 178, fols. 34v–35r, Hayne, De tous biem playne, i–x–x. Kassel, no. 13, ?– [superius partbook only]; the editor has been unable to consult this source. London 31922, fols. 40v–41r, anon, De tous bien plane, i–x–i; index: de tous bien playne. Maastricht, fols. 25r–25v, anon, De tous bin plaijn, r– [superius only].[6] Mellon, fols. 42v–43r, Heyne, De tous biens plaine, r–i–i. Monte Cassino, p. 344 (fol. 102Av), anon, textless, x–x–x. Paris 676, fols. 42v–43r, anon, De tous biens, i–i–i. Pavia 362, fols. 34*bis*v–35r, Heyne, De tous biens playne, i–i–x; probably a later addition to the manuscript since it is written in a hand different from that of the main scribe; the same condition obtains several folios later on 50v–51r where *Mon cuer de dueil* appears, also in a later hand. Perugia 431, no. 80, fols. 70v–71r, anon, De tous biens plaine est, i–i–i; Nanie Bridgman erroneously cites fols. 80v–81r; see idem, "Un Manuscrit italien du début du XVIe siècle à la Bibliothèque Nationale (Département de la Musique, Rés. Vm.[7] 676)," *Annales musicologiques* 1 (1953): 214–15. Pixérécourt, fols. 105v–106r, anon, De tous biens est plaine, r–i–i. Ricc 2356, fols. 32v–33r, anon, De tout bien pleine, x–i–i; omitted from index. Ricc 2794, fols. 18v–19r, anon, De tous biens plaine, r–x–x. Sev/P, fol. 39r, anon, De tous biens playne, ?–i–i [superius lost]; MS index incomplete. Ulm 237, discantus fol. 17r, tenor fol. 15r, bassus fol. 16r, anon, De tous biens plaine, i–x–x. Uppsala 76a, fols. 15v–16r, anon, [D]e tous biens plaine, i–i–i; concordance omitted from HayneOO. Wolfenbüttel, fols. 52v–53r, anon, De tous biens plaine, t–i–i.

Intabulations. Pesaro, pp. 65–68, no. 76, anon, De tus biense; preserves aspects of all three voices in an ornamented transformation. Note that intabulations in other sources are more remote. Spinacino 2, no. 9, fols. 16r–18v, Francesco Spinacino, De tous biens; this two-lute arrangement by Spinacino paraphrases the tenor. Capriola, fols. 20v–22r, anon, Detobiens plaene nel ton del primo recerchar; this "Recerchar" bears some motivic resemblance to the model, probably—but not definitely—the Hayne setting. Spinacino 1, no. 22, fols. 37v–38r, Francesco Spinacino, Ricercare de tous biens; this Spinacino recercare carries few aural reminders of the original. Fribourg, fols. 2r–2v, anon, De Toss bien; this setting was omitted from Brown and HayneOO, but identified by Jürg Stenzl, "Peter Falk und die Musik in Freiburg," *Schweizerische Musikzeitung* 121 (1981): 293–94; it has not been consulted here; in the description of the Fribourg source, however, Fallows observes that the Fribourg intabulation is close to the one in Pesaro; see Fallows, 37.

Non-concordant sources. Cop 1848, p. 201, ?, ?, –?–[tenor alone]; Dragan Plamenac erroneously claims this as a concordance for the Hayne setting (see idem, "A Postscript to 'The "Second" Chansonnier of the Biblioteca Riccardiana,'" *Annales musicologiques* 4 [1956]: 264); this setting is in fact part of an *a 3* quodlibet/combinative chanson *Venez Tretons* (Brown nn, HayneOO 19, Meconi 6v); Hayne's tenor appears as the middle voice and is supplied with the full refrain text. Formschneider, no. 60; HayneOO lists source as containing Hayne's setting under its heading in the source list, but not in the concordance list; the version discussed is actually setting 16. Mun 239, fols. 15v–16r, anon, textless, x–x–x–[x]; actually setting 8.

David Fallows believes, with some justification, that the isolated partbook superius lines in Egenolff and in Kassel "are almost certainly from the setting by Ghiselin"; see Fallows, 129. They might equally well be copies of other superius-based settings of the work, however, for a number of such settings circulated in print. Since their identity is uncertain, they are listed here as concordances to the Hayne setting, but that attribution is uncertain at best.

Comments

An extensive discussion of the Franco-Burgundian transmission of this piece can be found in Duff James Kennedy, "Six Chansonniers Français: The Central Sources of the Franco-Burgundian Chanson" (Ph.D. diss., University of California at Santa Barbara, 1986), 473–79. Signatures and placement of accidentals vary from source to source. Most sources have B♭ in all three voices. Five sources also have E♭ in the tenor: Cop 291/8, Cordiforme, Dijon, Paris 676, and Perugia 431. Six sources include an E♭ in the contratenor: Laborde, Cop 291/8, Dijon, London 31922, Perugia 431, and Uppsala 76a. Four sources have no accidentals in the signature for the contratenor: Cordiforme, Monte Cassino, Paris 676, Pavia 362.

Some sources include cautionary flats in the superius part, confirming the readings of Laborde. Paris 676 gives a flat for measure 7, note 1 (compensating for the absence of an upper B♭ in the signature on this system); for measure 17, note 1, a cautionary flat appears in Bologna Q16, Cop 291/8, Pavia 362, and Ricc 2356; and for measure 54, note 1, there is a cautionary flat in Cop 291/8 and Pavia 362.

In several sources, the tenor lacks one or two flats found in Laborde which, however, could be easily derived through the rule of "una nota super la semper est canendum fa" (one note above la is always sung as fa). In measure 8, note 1, the flat is omitted in Casanatense, Cape Town, Ricc 2356, Sev/P, Ulm 237, Uppsala 76a, and Wolfenbüttel; in measure 54, note 2, the flat is omitted in Bologna Q16, Flor 121, Ricc 2356, Ricc 2794, Ulm 237, Uppsala 76a, and Wolfenbüttel.

Understandably, the most complicated picture obtains with the contratenor, reflecting the variable key signatures and, presumably, scribal initiative. Those sources lacking accidentals in the signature might be expected to have the greatest number of notated accidentals within the voice part, but this is, in fact, not necessarily true. All four sources have at least one accidental, but Cordiforme and Pav 362 only provide a single E♭ for measure 5, note 1, and Monte Cassino only indicates the B♭ for measure 11, note 1. These single accidentals may have functioned in a manner similar to signatures, cautioning the performer of the general harmonic range of the piece. Only Paris 676 gives much detail in its accidentals, and it is inconsistent, including the flats in measure 11, note 1; measure 15, note 1; and measure 43, note 2, but omitting the flat of measure 5, note 1, and measure 13, note 1, for instance.

The manuscripts with both B♭ and E♭ in the contratenor signature have relatively few accidentals. London 31922 includes a cautionary B♭ for measure 43, note 2; Perugia 431 includes a redundant E♭ for measure 5, note 1, and probably the B♭ of measure 43, note 2, though the positioning of the latter accidental on the G space prior to the rest at the start of measure 42 is somewhat problematic.

The final cluster of sources contain only B♭ in the signatures and tend to sprinkle only occasional accidentals elsewhere. Bologna Q16 includes the E♭ for measure 15, note 1. Cape Town includes the E♭ for measure 11, note 1; measure 13, note 1; measure 15, note 1; and measure 43, note 2. Pixérécourt includes flats for measure 5, note 1; measure 11, note 1; and measure 43, note 2. Ricc 2794 includes the flat for measure 5, note 1.

This variable treatment of accidentals shows that the contratenor harmonies at the beginning of the setting are relatively unambiguous: most readings include E♭ up through measure 15, although the placement of the cautionary accidental in measure 15, rather than two bars earlier, might indicate a temporary hexachoradal shift in some sources. Later in the setting, the harmonic language seems to be more open to interpretation, and the contratenor's E♭s in measures 32, 34, and 54 may be raised at the performer's discretion.

NOTES

M. 1, CT, note 1 through m. 2, note 2 is replaced by long G (or its rhythmic equivalent) in Casanatense, Cordiforme, Flor 121, Flor 178, London 31922, Ricc 2356, and Ulm 237. M. 5, CT, notes 1–2 are replaced by br G in Paris 676. M. 5, CT, note 2 is d in Flor 121. M. 7, S, notes 1–3 are sbr–min–min in Bologna Q16. M. 7, CT, note 1 through m. 8, note 1 is replaced by dotted sbr d–min c–min c–min B♭ in Bologna Q16; the same substitution occurs an octave higher at m. 11, note 1 through m. 12, note 1. M. 11, CT, notes 1–2 are dotted sbr b♭–min a in Wolfenbüttel. M. 11, CT, note 2 is replaced by min rest–min b♭ in all concordant sources except Cop 291/8, Dijon, Perugia 431, Ricc 2794, and Wolfenbüttel; Monte Cassino includes the min rest but maintains a sbr b♭, creating a rhythmic error. M. 16, CT, note 4 is A in Bologna Q16, Cordiforme, Paris 676. M. 20, CT, note 1 is e in Pavia 362. M. 31, CT, note 1 is B♭ in Uppsala 76a. M. 31, CT, note 1 is e in Wolfenbüttel. M. 32, S, note 2 through m. 33, note 2 is replaced by dotted sbr g′–sbr f′–min e′ in Ulm 237. M. 35, S, note 2 through m. 36, note 1 is replaced by br c′ in nearly all concordant sources; only Cop 291/8, Dijon, and Wolfenbüttel support Laborde's reading. M. 36, CT, note 3 is e in London 31922. M. 39, CT, note 1 is d in Flor 121, Flor 178, Ricc 2356. M. 39, CT, note 1 through m. 41, note 2 is replaced by sbr d–sbr G–br d–br G in Cape Town, CG, Mellon, Paris 676, Pavia 362, Perugia 431, Pixérécourt, and Uppsala 76a. M. 40, CT, note 1 through m. 43, note 2 has a copying error in Bologna Q16: m. 40, note 1 through m. 42, note 2 were initially omitted, and a custos now cues the reader to the addition; m. 43, notes 1–2 are replaced by br g in this reading. M. 41, CT, notes 1–2 are replaced by br G in London 31922. M. 42, CT, note 2 through m. 43, note 2 are replaced by dotted br g (or its rhythmic equivalent) in Cordiforme, Flor 121, Flor 178, Monte Cassino, Ricc 2356, Ricc 2794, and Ulm 237. M. 43, T, note 1, a bar line precedes the rest in Ricc 2356. M. 43, CT, notes 1–2 are replaced by dotted sbr g–min e in Uppsala 76a. M. 46, CT, note 1 through end is lacking in Mellon. M. 48, CT, note 2 is e in Casanatense, CG, Pavia 362. M. 50, S, note 2 is min in Laborde; c″ colored sbr–b♭′ min in Maastrict. M. 50, S, note 2 through m. 51, note 4 is min–min–sbr–min–min in Cop 291/8 and Dijon. M. 51, S, note 1 is b♭′ in Bologna Q16. M. 52, CT, note 1 is B♭ in Ulm 237. M. 57, S, notes 2–3 are dotted sbr–min in Maastricht. M. 58, T, notes 1–2 are dotted sbr–min in Ricc 2356. M. 59, CT is given elaborate cadential ornamentation in CG. M. 60, corona is provided for all parts in London 31922 and Ulm 237 and for S in Cape Town.

2. *De tous biens playne*
Anonymous
a 4; retains S, T, CT

Inventory numbers. Brown d1; HayneOO 6b; Meconi 2.

SOURCE

Primary source. Odhecaton, no. 20, fols. 22v–23r, anon, De tous biens playne, i–i–i–i; index: De tous biens. Altus labeled "si placet."

NOTE

M. 36, B, note 3 is e.

3. *[De tous biens plaine]*
Anonymous
a 4; retains [S?], [T?], CT

Inventory number. Meconi 6o.

SOURCE

Primary source. Bologna Q18, fol. 48r (47v lacking in source), anon, textless, [?]–x–[?]–x. Only a new altus and the Hayne contratenor survive.

COMMENTS

The setting may have had a modified or re-composed superius, as most of the conflicts, and particularly the clash at measure 57, note 1 and measure 58, note 2, are between altus of Bologna Q18 and Hayne's superius. Nevertheless, the adoption of a borrowed tenor-contratenor pair without the accompanying superius is unheard of elsewhere in the repertory, and the editor has judged this to be an *a 4* rendition, supplying the superius and tenor voices from the Hayne original.

NOTES

M. 16, B, note 2 is A. M. 21, A, note 1 is f. M. 57, A, note 1 through m. 58, note 2 is br a–sbr a–min g.

4. *De tous biens playne*
Anonymous
a 3; retains S, T

Inventory numbers. Brown i; HayneOO 5; Meconi 3b.

SOURCE

Primary source. Flor Panc 27, no. 36, fol. 25r, anon, De tous biens playne, i–x–x.

COMMENTS

The piece was evidently proofread, for the number 118 (which indicates the length of the piece in semibreve units, excluding from this tally the final long) appears next to the final bar line in each part. There are several awkward spots in the setting. Parallel octaves and fifths appear between the cantus and contra in measures 18–19, 26, 31, 39, and 49, and between tenor and contra in measures 21–22 and 32–33. Empty harmonies also occur; in the first phrase, hollow perfect fifths appear in measures 2 and 5. Finally, the style of this setting seems anachronistic, for the contra employs octave-leap cadences and displays the general leaping contour characteristic of the early to mid-fifteenth century.

5. *De tous biens plaine*

Anonymous
a 3; retains S, T

Inventory numbers. Brown h; HayneOO 4; Meconi 3a.

SOURCE

Primary source. Banco Rari 229, fols. 187v–188r [no. 177], anon, De tous biens plaine, r–x–x.

COMMENTS

Heavy use of ligatures in the tenor conflicts with text placement; the scribe may have expected untexted performance. The editor has ignored ligatures in suggesting a possible texting for this voice.

6. *De tous biens*

Anonymous
a 3; retains S, T

Inventory numbers. Brown j; HayneOO 6; Meconi 3c.

SOURCE

Primary source. Canti C, no. 118, fols. 143v–144r, anon, De tous biens, i–i–i.

NOTES

M. 25, CT, note 2 is g. M. 37, CT, note 2 through m. 39, note 1 is corrupt: the long rest (whole rest) provided there would leave a gap of a measure in transcription; the editor has changed the long rest to a sbr rest and repeated the motive that follows.

7. *De tous bien*

de Planquard
a 4; retains S, T

Inventory numbers. Brown g; HayneOO 3; Meconi 4a.

SOURCE

Primary source. Banco Rari 229, fols. 188v–189r [no. 178], de Planquard, De tous bien, i–i–i–[i].

COMMENTS

Only the part for contratenor 1 is included in the source. Contratenor 2 has been derived from the canon "fuga de minima" written in the left-hand margin of folio 189r. Awkward harmonies, mostly a minim in length but rarely resolved, occur frequently on weak beats. These appear to be motivated by the two-fold goals of keeping the strong beats consonant and maintaining the rhythmic activity. See, for example, measure 18, contratenor 1, note 6 and measure 19, note 5, both of which establish a consonant downbeat for contratenor 2 in the following measure.

NOTE

M. 59, CT 1, note 4 is min rest–min d–long g (as shown in m. 59, CT 2, notes 6–7 and m. 60) with a *signum congruentiae* over the min rest to mark the cadential arrival, but no alternate ending is supplied; the solution provided is the same one proposed by Howard Mayer Brown in his edition of Banco Rari 229; see *A Florentine Chansonnier from the Time of Lorenzo the Magnificent: Florence, Biblioteca Nazionale Centrale MS Banco Rari 229*, Monuments of Renaissance Music, vol. 7 (Chicago: University of Chicago Press, 1983), 2:407.

8. *[De tous biens plaine]*

[Josquin des Prez]
a 4; retains S, T

Inventory numbers. Brown f; HayneOO 2; Meconi 4b.

SOURCES

Primary source. Mun 239, fols. 15v–16r, anon, textless, x–x–x–[x]. Brown omits this source. This setting is incorrectly identified as Hayne van Ghizeghem (setting 1) in Clytus Gottwald, ed., *Die Musikhandschriften der Universitätsbibliothek, München* (Wiesbaden: Otto Harrassowitz, 1968), 101.

Concordant sources. Glareanus, pp. 452–53, Iodocus, textless, x–x–x–[x]. Odhecaton, no. 95, fols. 102v–103r; anon, De tous biens playne i–i–i–[i]; index: De tous biens, Josqn.

COMMENTS

Only the part for contratenor 1 is included in the primary source and the concordant sources. The canon is lacking in the primary source, but the upper margin of this manuscript has been extensively trimmed, and the descenders of one or possibly two letters remain. Glareanus labels the contratenor "Fuga ad minimam," and *Odhecaton* follows the contratenor with the text "Canon Petrus e[t] Joannes currunt In puncto."

NOTES

M. 19, CT 1, note 4 through m. 20, note 2 and m. 20, CT 2, notes 1–2, the dotted min–smin is repeated in *Odhecaton*. M. 57, CT 1, note 1 and CT 2, note 2 are c in all sources. M. 60, CT 1, note 5 through m. 61, note 3 and m. 61, CT 2, notes 1–3 are lacking in Mun 239 and have been supplied from *Odhecaton*.

9. *De tobiens plena*

Anonymous
a 3; retains S

Inventory numbers. Brown e; HayneOO 27; Meconi 6d.

SOURCE

Primary source. CG, fols. 57v–58r (64v–65r), anon, De tobiens plena, i–x–x; index: De To biens plaine. The superius is shared with the Hayne setting found on the same opening. Brown and others incorrectly identify this as part of a setting *a 5*. Allan Atlas determined that the opening contains two discrete settings which share the superius part; see idem, *The Cappella Giulia Chansonnier: Rome, Biblioteca Apostolica Vaticana, C.G.XIII.27,* Musicological Studies, vol. 27 (Brooklyn: Institute of Mediaeval Music, 1975), 1:137–39.

COMMENT

A series of bar lines in the tenor indicates the repetition of each motive in turn.

10. *De tous biens*

Josquin [des Prez]
a 3; retains S

Inventory numbers. Brown o; HayneOO 26; Meconi 6m.

SOURCE

Primary source. Motetti A, fol. 55v, Josquin [placed over T], De tous biens, i–x–[x]; index: De tous biens. Josquin.

COMMENTS

The source labels the tenor part "Tenor et Contra" in the left-hand margin. The contra has been derived from the instruction "Canon. Fuga per semibrevem in netesinemenon:" written above the notation.

11. *De tous biens*

[Johannes] Ghiselin [*dit* Verbonnet]
a 3; retains S

Inventory numbers. Brown n; HayneOO 24; Meconi 6n.

SOURCES

Primary source. Canti B, no. 42, fols. 45v–46r, Ghiselin, De tous biens, i–x–i; index: De tous biens. Ghiselin.

Intabulation. Arrangement for solo lute, Newsidler, no. 9, Ghiselin. Tus Biens. This arrangement is listed in Brown, *Instrumental Music Printed Before 1600: A Bibliography* (Cambridge, MA: Harvard University Press, 1965), 53–55. HayneOO, however, incorrectly claims that this is an intabulation of Josquin's *Credo De tous biens plaine,* HayneOO 47.

Non-concordant sources. Egenolff, though listed by GhiselinOO as a concordance (under the abbreviation Paris ... res. Vm^7 504), in fact provides only the superius since the other partbooks are missing; it has been listed here as a concordance to the original Hayne setting. Fallows, 129, suggests that Kassel too might be a concordance to Ghiselin's setting, but it also provides only the superius in a single partbook copy and has likewise been included in this edition as a concordance to the original Hayne setting. Schöffer, Liederbuch, 1513, Nr. 42, cited in GhiselinOO, is apparently a phantom; the source [Songbook], (Mainz: P. Schöffer, 1513 [RISM 1513^2]), does not, in fact, contain any settings of *De tous biens plaine.* GhiselinOO incorrectly lists Capirola as having a concordant intabulation.

12. *De tous biens playne*

Anonymous
a 4; retains S

Inventory numbers. Brown l; HayneOO 22; Meconi 6r.

SOURCE

Primary source. Canti C, no. 66, fols. 88v–89r, anon, De tous biens planye [*sic*], i–i–i–i.

NOTE

M. 5, S, note 1, the incipit is "planye."

13. *[De tous biens plaine]*

Anonymous
a 3; retains S

Inventory numbers. Brown k; HayneOO 28; Meconi 6a.

SOURCE

Primary source. Mun 3154, no. 31, fols. 49v–50r, anon, textless, x–x–x.

NOTES

M. 29, S, note 1, the scribe jumped to m. 40, note 1 through m. 55, note 1, realized the mistake, hatched out the phrase, started again and copied m. 40, note 1 through m. 51, note 4, crossed it out, then copied the music supplied here. M. 33, S, note 1, the dot has been struck through by a later hand.   M. 42, CT, note 2, the b♭ min is repeated.   M. 50, CT, notes 1–2 are c–B♭.

14. *De tous biens*
Anonymous
a 4; retains S with some variation

Inventory numbers. Brown m; HayneOO 23; Meconi 6s.

SOURCE

Primary source. Canti C, no. 84, fols. 110v–111r, anon, De tous biens, i–i–i–i.

COMMENTS

This setting appears with an attribution to Busnois in Rafael Georg Kiesewetter, musical supplement to "Die Verdienste der Niederländer um die Tonkunst," in *Verhandelingen over de vraag: Welke verdiensten habben zich de Nederlanders vooral in de 14e, 15e en 16e eeuw in het vak der toonkunst verworven* (Amsterdam: J. Muller en comp., 1829), 58–60. According to Kiesewetter's comments, the setting was edited from a copy of *Canti C* in Vienna. The setting lacks attribution in the known surviving copies, however, and is unlikely to belong to the Busnois canon.

NOTE

M. 56, T, note 1 is dotted sbr.

15. *[De tous biens plaine]*
Anonymous
a 3; retains T

Inventory numbers. Brown v; HayneOO 18; Meconi 6l.

SOURCE

Primary source. Verona 757, fols. 43v–44r, anon, textless, x–x–x.

COMMENTS

The bassus shares initial motivic material with settings 16, 17a, and 17b. Brown erroneously claims that it shares the entire bassus of 17b. A modern hand has entered "De tous biens plaine" next to the tenor cantus firmus.

NOTES

M. 20, T, note 2 through m. 21, note 2 are inserted in the manuscript, having initially been omitted.   M. 22, T, note 3 is followed by an erasure in source; m. 21, note 2 through m. 22, note 2 were mistakenly copied twice at the end of the line.   M. 23, B, note 4 is followed by an erasure, perhaps of two semiminims. M. 36, B, note 2 is followed by ♭.

16. *De tobiens plaine e ma maetressa*
Anonymous
a 3; retains T

Inventory numbers. Brown z; HayneOO 17; Meconi 6c.

SOURCES

Primary source. CG, fols. 17v–18r (24v–25r), anon, De tobiens plaine e ma maetressa, i–x–x; index: De To biens playne.

Concordant sources. Canti C, no. 117, fols. 142v–143r, anon, De tous biens playne, i–i–i. Formschneider, no. 60, anon, textless but with handwritten incipit "De tous biens playne" in the tenor partbook of the Jena copy, x–i–x; index: De tous biens.

COMMENTS

The superius shares initial motivic material with settings 17a and 17b. The bassus shares initial motivic material with settings 15, 17a, and 17b. In general, *Canti C* and Formschneider provide more ornamentation than CG, filling in leaps and providing more elaborate ornaments at cadences. The *Canti C* and Formschneider readings also prefer syncopation in lieu of rhythmic repetition (in S, m. 32, note 3 through m. 33, note 3; m. 47, note 3 through m. 48, note 1; and m. 49, notes 2–3; in T, m. 20, note 2 through m. 21, note 1, and m. 53, note 2 through m. 54, note 1; and in B, m. 16, note 4 through m. 17, note 1). These differences may well reflect the preferences of the compositors for traditional rhythmic treatment or the idiosyncratic preferences of the CG scribe for clear-cut strong beats.

NOTES

B is labeled "Contra" in *Canti C*.   M. 2, B, notes 3–4 are replaced by sbr c in *Canti C* and Formschneider.   M. 8, T, note 1 is ♭ in *Canti C* and Formschneider. M. 12, S, note 3 is d' in Formschneider.   Mm. 15–16, 41–42, 47–48, T, use longs instead of repeated breves in *Canti C* and Formschneider. Mm. 13–18, T, Formschneider offers a three-note ligature for this cadential passage; in mm. 15–17, the typesetter evidently intended a perfect long for the br–br–sbr rest–sbr of the primary source; Formschneider's reading is defective, however, for a tail on the ligature transforms the intended dotted long into a dotted br.   M. 17, B, note 3, *Canti C* supplies ♭ but ambiguously places it on the F line, suggesting a forced e-mi; the cadential preparation, however, suggests an e-fa interpretation; Formschneider supports the latter reading, providing e♭. M. 18, T, note 1 is omitted in Formschneider.   M. 20, B, note 3 is a sbr d in *Canti C* and Formschneider.   M. 21, S, notes 4–5 appear to be colored sbr e'–min d′–min a in CG; the reading is unclear, and a void sbr e′ may be beneath the first two notes of the figure; the editor has substituted the reading from *Canti C*. M. 21, T, note 2 through m. 22, note 3 is a two-br ligature c′–d′ in Formschneider. M. 22, T, notes 1–3 are replaced with br d′ in *Canti C* and Formschneider. M. 26, B, note 2 is ♭ in *Canti C* and Formschneider. M. 28, B, note 1 is A♭ in *Canti C*, perhaps following the una nota supra la rule, but this would provoke a cross-relation with the superius; Formschneider provides a b♭ for m. 28, note 7, suggesting that *Canti C* may have misplaced a warning accidental. M. 32, S, note 3 through m. 33, note 3 are br g′–min f′–min e′ in *Canti C* and Formschneider. M. 32, B, note 5 lacks ♭ in *Canti C* and Formschneider. M. 39, B, note 2 lacks ♭ in *Canti C*; Formschneider supplies ♭. M. 46, B, note 2 is e♭ in Formschneider. M. 47, S, note 3 through m. 48, note 1 and m. 49, notes 2–3 are replaced by a dotted min in *Canti C* and Formschneider. Mm. 53–55, S, the cadential preparations in *Canti C* and Formschneider leading to m. 53, note 3 and m. 55, note 1 are more ornamented than those in CG and create a musical parallel with the cadential figures of mm. 56–58. M. 53, S, note 4 is b♭ in Formschneider. M. 54, B, note 4 is ♭ in Formschneider. M. 54, T, note 2 is ♭ in *Canti C* and Formschneider. M. 55, B, note 2 is ♭ in *Canti C*. M. 57, B, note 3 is A in Formschneider. M. 58, S, notes 1–2 are replaced by a dotted min b♭ in Formschneider. M. 59, S, note 1 is replaced by smin f′–smin d′ in *Canti C* and Formschneider. M. 60, B, note 1 lacks ♭ in *Canti C*. M. 62, B, note 1 is replaced by sbr rest–sbr G in Formschneider.

17a. *De tous biens*

[Alexander] Agricola
a 4; retains T

Inventory numbers. Brown u; HayneOO 9; Meconi 6e.

Source

Primary source. Canti C, no. 62, fols. 83v–84r, Agricola, De tous biens, i–i–i.

Comments

The superius shares initial motivic material with setting 16, and the bassus shares initial motivic material with settings 15 and 16. This setting also incorporates all three voices found in setting 17b. It is probable that the four-voice version from *Canti C* is the original and the three-voice version in Ver and CG (setting 17b) a reduction. Both settings are musically successful, but the coherence of the contra line unique to the *Canti C* setting and its stylistic resemblance to the rest of the polyphonic complex suggests that a single composer conceived of all four voices.

Notes

M. 15, T, note 1 through m. 16, note 1, the long g is detached from the ligature. M. 20, CT, note 3 is a colored br.

17b. *[De tous biens plaine]*

[Alexander Agricola?]
a 3; retains T

Inventory numbers. Brown u; HayneOO 9; Meconi 6e.

Sources

Primary source. Verona 757, fols. 42v–43r, anon, textless, x–x–x. Brown mistakenly has 43v.

Concordant source. CG, fols. 70v–71r (77v–78r), anon, De to biens plaine, i–x–x; index: De to biens plena.

Comments

This setting shares motivic material with settings 15 and 16; see commentary for 17a on the relationship between the four-voice and three-voice versions of this work. The two sources for the three-voice version both present the work anonymously; the attribution to Agricola comes from the four-voice setting. A modern hand has supplied incipits for the superius ("De tous biens") and the tenor ("De tous biens pleine est ma maistresse") in Verona 757.

Notes

S lacks time signature in CG. M. 8, T, note 1 lacks ♭ in CG. M. 13, S, note 2 through m. 14, note 4 is ornamented in CG: a running smin figure replaces the syncopation. M. 22, T, note 2 through m. 24, note 1 are written as two minims and a three-note ligature at the end of the first system and then erroneously repeated as single notes at the start of the second system in Verona 757; the scribe caught the error and lined out the repetition with two horizontal strokes, adjusting the custos at the end of system 1 to reflect the change. M. 37, B, note 1 lacks ♭ in CG.

18. *De tous biens*

Anonymous
a 3; retains T

Inventory number. Meconi 6f.

Source

Primary source. Bologna Q16, fols. 137(a)v–138(a)r, anon, De tous biens plein, i–i–i.

Comments

The setting has been suppressed by gluing the pages together. This suppression occurred before the roman-numeral enumeration of pieces and before the entry of initials (the superius lacks a *D* and the tenor and contratenor are unlabeled), but after yellow wash was added to the tenor's capital *D* and to the dots showing truncation of the text. Pease noted the presence of the incipit on the glued pages in his inventory of Bologna Q16, but did not further identify the piece; see Edward Pease, "A Report on Codex Q16 of the Civico Museo Bibliografico Musicale," *Musica Disciplina* 20 (1966): 76.

To transcribe this piece, the editor derived information from bleed-through and from a backlit view of the interior. Since four layers of music were superimposed over one another (the recto 137 and its matching—and suppressed—verso 137a, and the suppressed interior 138a recto and its exterior verso 138), the reading is not always certain, but every effort has been taken to double-check the spots which are harmonically or melodically corrupt. Note that the superius in particular is corrupt in the source, which may have motivated the suppression of the piece.

NOTES

M. 5, S, note 1 lacks dot. M. 8, B, note 3, dot is clear; note and value are not. M. 10, S, notes 7–8 are added by editor; an alternate solution would be to change m. 10, notes 5–6 to minims. M. 14, B, note 2 through m. 16, note 1, the reading is uncertain; it is obscured by the *C* of contra on the outer page; m. 14, note 2 appears to be a sbr. M. 18, S, note 2 is added by the editor. M. 23, S, note 6, the pitch is ambiguous in source; scribe has extended the notehead to cover both the pitches a' and g'. M. 29, S, note 2 is sbr. M. 30, T, note 1 may be lacking in source. M. 33, S, note 3 is added by the editor. M. 41, S, note 1 is added by the editor. M. 50, B, note 2, pitch for first note of the c.o.p. ligature is ambiguous; could be c or B♭. M. 55, S, note 1, the dissonant ninth with B could be avoided by changing a' to b♭'.

19. De tous biens

Bourdon/[Alexander Agricola]
a 3; retains T

Inventory numbers. Brown aa; HayneOO 15; Meconi 6g.

SOURCES

Primary source. Odhecaton, no. 73, fols. 79v–80r, anon, De tous biens, i–i–i; index: De tous bie[n]s: Bourdo[n].

Concordant source. Segovia, fol. 173v, Alexander agricola, De tous biens playne, i–i–i. This concordance was omitted by Brown and Hewitt.

COMMENTS

Proper attribution for this work remains an open question; the setting is, however, less motivically obsessive than the other Agricola settings which draw on *De tous biens plaine*, so a slight preference might be given to Bourdon. Several errors appear in the contra of Segovia, but most of the differences are of ornamentation.

NOTES

M. 4, S, notes 2–3 are simplified to min e' in Segovia. M. 7, S, note 4 through m. 8, note 1 are sbr d'–min c' in Segovia. M. 8, T, note 1 is ♭ in Segovia. M. 9, S, note 4 through m. 10, note 2 is simplified to sbr b♭' in Segovia. M. 19, CT, notes 1–2 are min–sbr in Segovia. M. 23, CT, note 1, sbr lacking in Segovia. M. 24, S, note 2 through m. 25, note 1 is replaced by a dotted sbr in Segovia. M. 26, S, note 5 is g in Segovia. M. 27, CT, notes 1–2 are two minims in Segovia. M. 33, CT, notes 2–3 are B♭–c in Segovia. M. 36, S, note 3 through m. 37, note 1 are dotted min–smin in Segovia. M. 44, CT, note 2 is e in Segovia. M. 44, S, note 4 through m. 45, note 1 was entered as min and then changed to sbr in Segovia. M. 48, CT, note 4 through m. 51, note 4 have an alternate reading in Segovia. M. 52, S, note 1 was entered as min and then changed to sbr in Segovia. M. 57, T, notes 1–2 are a c.o.p. ligature in Segovia.

20. De tous biens playne

Alexander Agricola
a 3; retains T

Inventory numbers. Brown dd; HayneOO 12; Meconi 6h.

SOURCES

Primary source. Segovia, fols. 180v–181r (Brown mistakenly has 174v), Alexander agrico[la],[7] De tous biens playne, i–i–i.

Non-concordant source. Perugia 1013, fol. 136v. Brown mistakenly lists "Per 1013 f. 136v" as a concordance for this setting, but it is in fact setting 23.

21. De tous biens playne

Alexander Agricola
a 3; retains T

Inventory numbers. Brown ee; HayneOO 13; Meconi 6i.

SOURCE

Primary source. Segovia, fols. 194v–195r, Alexander agrico[la],[8] De tous biens playne, i–i–i. Brown mistakenly has 188v and erroneously claims the setting is *a 2*; AgricOO mistakenly has 193v–195r.

22. *De tous biens playne*

Allexander [Agricola]
a 3; retains T

Inventory numbers. Brown bb; HayneOO 10; Meconi 6u.

SOURCE

Primary source. Flor C 2439, fols. 67v–68r, Allexander, De tous biens playne, i–i–i; index: De touus [*sic*] biens: Alex.

NOTE

M. 13, B, note 2 is c.

23. *De tous biens playne*

Allexander [Agricola]
a 3; retains T

Inventory numbers. Brown cc; HayneOO 11; Meconi 6t.

SOURCES

Primary source. Flor C 2439, fols. 66v–67r, Allexander, De tous biens playne, i–i–i; index: De touus [*sic*] biens: Alex.

Concordant source. Perugia 1013, fols. 136v–137r, Agricola, textless, x–x–x. Brown mistakes this setting as a concordance for setting 20; AgricOO and Hewitt both identify the setting correctly.

NOTES

M. 23, B, note 6 lacks ♭ in Perugia 1013. M. 26, B, note 5 has a scribal correction in Perugia 1013: a br has been changed to a sbr. M. 37, S, note 5 is b♭' in Perugia 1013. M. 42, S, note 1 is sbr d'–min rest in Perugia 1013. M. 49, S, note 4 is b♭' in Perugia 1013. M. 52, S, note 3, d' is overwritten by the scribe to read e' in Flor C 2439. M. 52, B, note 4 lacks ♭ in Perugia 1013. M. 53, B, note 1 has a scribal correction in Perugia 1013: d has been changed to c. M. 54, T, note 2 lacks ♭ in Perugia 1013.

24. *De tous biens*

Bactio [Bartolomeo degli Organi]
a 3; retains T

Inventory numbers. Brown x; HayneOO 14; Meconi 6j.

SOURCE

Primary source. Bologna Q17, fols. 26v–27r, Bactio, De tous biens, i–x–x.

COMMENTS

The attribution is discussed by Richard Wexler, "Newly Identified Works by Bartolomeo degli Organi in the MS Bologna Q17," *Journal of the American Musicological Society* 23 (1970): 107–18, esp. 107. The tenor part appears to be signed "el servo povero se'rv' d' dio."

NOTES

M. 9, B, notes 4–7, flags have been lined out. M. 59, B, note 2 is dotted sbr.

25. *De to biens playne*

Anonymous
a 3; retains T, but augments it

Inventory numbers. Brown y; HayneOO 16; Meconi 6b.

SOURCE

Primary source. CG, fols. 15v–17r (22v–24r), anon, De to biens playne, i–x–x; index: De tous biens plaine.

COMMENT

Tenor canon: "Crescit in duplo."

NOTES

M. 34, B, notes 4–6, triplet indicated by "3." M. 63, S, notes 3–6, noteheads missing in source; remaining stems indicate the reading supplied here. M. 94, S, notes 4–5 are b♭–a. M. 96, S, notes 4–5 are b♭'–a'.

26. *De tous bien plen*

Anonymous
a 4; retains T but transposes it up a fifth and places it in the superius

Inventory numbers. Brown r; HayneOO 20; Meconi 6p.

SOURCE

Primary source. Bologna Q18, fols. 51v–52r, anon, De tous bien plen, i–x–x–x.

27. *De tous biens*

Jo[hannes] Japart
a 4; retains T but inverts it and places it in the contra

Inventory numbers. Brown t; HayneOO 7; Meconi 6q.

SOURCE

Primary source. Canti C, no. 59, fols. 79v–80r, Jo. Japart, De tous biens, i–i–i–i.

COMMENTS

The contra gives the traditional Hayne tenor melody which must be transposed and inverted following the instructions that appear above the music: "Canon. Hic can[i]tur antipodes" (This is sung upside down). The tenor incipit is misplaced in source; it appears beneath the final system of the superius part.

NOTES

M. 15, CT, note 1, pitch is separated from the ligature.   M. 22, S, note 3 is min.

28. De tous biens plaine

D'Oude Schuere
a 4; retains T but transposes and varies it

Inventory numbers. Brown s; HayneOO 8; Meconi 6w.

SOURCE

Primary source. Cambrai 125–28, no. 27, fol. 46v, D'Oude Schuere, De tous biens plaine, i–i–i–i.

COMMENTS

The superius and contratenor end with the word "finis." The mistress depicted in the historiated initial of the tenor is not, perhaps, full of such good virtue, as she and her partner are both naked and preparing for an obviously carnal embrace.

Notes

1. Wolfgang Boetticher, *Handschriftlich überlieferte Lauten- und Gitarrentabulaturen des 15. bis 18. Jahrhunderts,* series B/7 of *Répertoire international des sources musicales* [RISM] (Munich: G. Henle, 1978), 79.
2. See Jürg Stenzl, "Peter Falk und die Musik in Freiburg," *Schweizerische Musikzeitung* 121 (1981): 294.
3. The editor has been unable to consult this source.
4. The dating is the editor's. The manuscript could easily stem from the later 1480s based on repertory alone, but if it is of German provenance, which seems probable, it is likely to have been copied slightly later. Martin Staehelin is preparing a study of the fragments.

5. Boetticher, *Handschriftlich überlieferte Lauten- und Gitarrentabulaturen,* 283.
6. The fourth word of the incipit is illegible in the facsimile and has been taken from Jozef Smits van Waesberghe, "Een 15de Eeuws Muziekboek van de Stadsminstrelen van Maastricht?" in *Renaissance-muziek 1400–1600: Donum natalicium René Bernard Lenaerts,* ed. Jozef Robijns, Musicologica Lovaniensia, vol. 1 (Louvain: Katholieke Universiteit, Seminarie voor Muziekwetenschap, 1969), 255.
7. The attribution uses the rebus ╬ for "-la."
8. The attribution uses the rebus ╬ for "-la."

RECENT RESEARCHES IN THE MUSIC OF THE MIDDLE AGES
AND EARLY RENAISSANCE
Charles M. Atkinson, general editor

Vol.	Composer: Title
1	Johannes Martini: *Secular Pieces*
2–3	*The Montpellier Codex. Part I: Critical Commentary; Fascicles 1 and 2*
4–5	*The Montpellier Codex. Part II: Fascicles 3, 4, and 5*
6–7	*The Montpellier Codex. Part III: Fascicles 6, 7, and 8*
8	*The Montpellier Codex. Part IV: Texts and Translations*
9–10	Johannes Vincenet: *The Collected Works*
11–13	*The Conductus Collections of MS Wolfenbüttel 1099*
14	*Fors seulement: Thirty Compositions for Three and Five Voices or Instruments from the Fifteenth and Sixteenth Centuries*
15	Johannes Cornago: *Complete Works*
16–18	*Beneventanum Troporum Corpus I. Tropes of the Proper of the Mass from Southern Italy, A.D. 1000–1250*
19–21	*Beneventanum Troporum Corpus II. Ordinary Chants and Tropes for the Mass from Southern Italy, A.D. 1000–1250. Part 1: Kyrie eleison*
22–24	*Beneventanum Troporum Corpus II. Ordinary Chants and Tropes for the Mass from Southern Italy, A.D. 1000–1250. Part 2: Gloria in excelsis*
25–26	*Beneventanum Troporum Corpus II. Ordinary Chants and Tropes for the Mass from Southern Italy, A.D. 1000–1250. Part 3: Preface Chants and Sanctus*
27	*Beneventanum Troporum Corpus II. Ordinary Chants and Tropes for the Mass from Southern Italy, A.D. 1000–1250. Part 4: Agnus Dei* [Not yet published.]
28	*Beneventanum Troporum Corpus III. Indexes, Inventories, and Analytical Studies* [Not yet published.]
29	*The Florence Laudario: An Edition of Florence, Biblioteca Nazionale Centrale, Banco Rari 18*
30	*Early Medieval Chants from Nonantola. Part I: Ordinary Chants and Tropes*
31	*Early Medieval Chants from Nonantola. Part II: Proper Chants and Tropes*
32	*Early Medieval Chants from Nonantola. Part III: Processional Chants*
33	*Early Medieval Chants from Nonantola. Part IV: Sequences*
34	Johannes Martini: *Masses. Part 1: Masses without Known Polyphonic Models*
35	Johannes Martini: *Masses. Part 2: Masses with Known Polyphonic Models*
36	*De tous biens plaine: Twenty-Eight Settings of Hayne van Ghizeghem's Chanson*